Walking with
Old Testament
Women

Text copyright © Fiona Stratta 2014
The author asserts the moral right
to be identified as the author of this work

Published by
The Bible Reading Fellowship
15 The Chambers, Vineyard
Abingdon OX14 3FE
United Kingdom
Tel: +44 (0)1865 319700
Email: enquiries@brf.org.uk
Website: www.brf.org.uk
BRF is a Registered Charity

ISBN 978 1 84101 718 1

First published 2014

10 9 8 7 6 5 4 3 2 1 0

Acknowledgements
Unless otherwise stated, scripture quotations are taken from the Holy Bible, New
Living Translation, copyright © 1996, 2004, 2007, 2013. Used by permission of
Tyndale House Publishers, Inc., Carol Stream, Illinois 60188. All rights reserved.

Scripture quotations taken from the Holy Bible, New International Version
(Anglicised edition), copyright © 1979, 1984, 2011 by Biblica. Used by permission
of Hodder & Stoughton Publishers, an Hachette UK company. All rights reserved.
'NIV' is a registered trademark of Biblica. UK trademark number 1448790.

Scripture quotations marked (ESV) are from the Holy Bible, English Standard
Version, published by HarperCollins Publishers, © 2001 Crossway Bibles, a
division of Good News Publishers. Used by permission. All rights reserved.

The Living Bible copyright © 1971 by Tyndale House Publishers.

Cover photo: Lisa Stirling/Photographer's Choice/Gettyimages.

A catalogue record for this book is available from the British Library

Printed and bound by CPI Group (UK) Ltd, Croydon CR0 4YY

Walking with
Old Testament
Women

Imaginative studies for Bible
meditation

FIONA STRATTA

Contents

Contents

Introduction

The following reflective monologues and studies are based on biblical accounts of women in the Old Testament, and are intended for groups who meet together to grow in their relationships with God and each other, or for individual use. The group should first read the Bible passage about the woman to be studied, followed by the monologue, which is written as if the woman herself is speaking.

There are several types of Christian meditation; one of them is to 'enter' scripture using the imagination. Superficially we may feel very different from these women who lived so long ago, but as we hear their stories we discover that we share much in common: joy and heartache; love and jealousy; difficult choices; the need for patience, wisdom and courage. We are not so dissimilar: in our society, too, there are dysfunctional families beset by difficulties, and many women across the world have little personal choice or freedom. Of greatest importance, we see in these narratives God's wonderful grace, his undeserved favour and blessing, touching the lives of these women, and we discover that this same grace is available to us.

Imaginative reflection on the Bible is not a new concept. It was practised by St Ignatius of Loyola in the 16th century. It can be a powerful way for God to speak to us, for this kind of meditation involves not only the mind but also the emotions. Jesus himself used imaginative narrative in the form of parables to engage with his listeners and thus to teach them effectively.

Although the monologues follow the biblical accounts accurately, not every detail will be true. After all, we are imagining, filling in the gaps with the possible. This need not be a problem, for it is precisely what we do when we tell Bible stories to children; we embellish the story to capture the child's imagination with the purpose of teaching spiritual truths.

Points for reflection and discussion follow the monologues, enabling issues to be explored and spiritual growth to take place. Links between the Old and New Testaments are made in each study, and we see how the Old Testament points to the coming of Jesus Christ. We experience the truth of Paul's words to Timothy, 'All scripture is inspired by God and is useful to teach us what is true and to make us realise what is wrong in our lives... God uses it to prepare and equip his people to do every good work' (2 Timothy 3:16–17). In some of the studies, verses are suggested for meditation: this involves a slow, deliberate and prayerful consideration of the verses, probing their depths. It allows scripture to work in us; we grow in our relationship with God as Father, Son and Holy Spirit.

Finally, there is the opportunity to record what God has been saying to us and the implications for our individual spiritual journeys. After all, in coming to God's word, we want not only to learn but also to change and to grow, so that we are not just 'hearers' of the word but 'doers'. The monologues can be used without the discussion element as a means of initiating a time of silent personal reflection or led meditation for a group. They can also stand alone effectively in many other contexts: for example, individuals can use them in private meditation, or they can be read to larger groups, such as congregations.

The facilitator

If you are the group facilitator, you will need to ensure that pens and paper are available, along with a variety of translations and paraphrases of the Bible. For the longer passages, you may need to select the passages to be read and the questions for discussion.

It will be your responsibility to introduce the study and to find someone to read the reflective monologue. Try to ask someone who is able to read aloud fluently and expressively.

You will need to read the links and facilitate the discussion, allowing enough time for personal reflection at the end. It may be helpful to play quiet music during the reflection.

Sarah (Part 1)

Introduction

- **Read Genesis 11:31–32; 12:1–5; 16:1–9, 15.**

- **Ask God to speak to you through this episode. You could use the words from 2 Corinthians 1:2: 'May God our Father and the Lord Jesus Christ give you grace and peace.'**

- **Sit back, relax and close your eyes. Imagine the scene as someone reads the monologue.**

Monologue

I had expected to feel nothing but relief as I saw Hagar and Ishmael walk away. Yes, I did feel an element of relief, but my feelings were far more complex than that. I felt guilty, for this whole situation had arisen through my wilful planning. I experienced a heaviness of heart, knowing that the man I loved was grieving profoundly as he watched his firstborn son disappear into the distance. Their absence would leave a gap in Abraham's life that I knew I could never fill, although our child, Isaac, would be a comfort and joy to him.

In the silence brought about by their departure, I fell to musing on the years that lay behind us, back to the time when we were known as Abram and Sarai. We started our life together in the fashionable and wealthy city of Ur and then moved with Abram's whole family to Haran. We had all the comforts of a prosperous urban life. My husband, unlike most of the men around us, had a deep faith in the God of his ancestors; he worshipped God with absolute devotion. Perhaps this was why God chose him and gave him the instructions that took us away from the stability of family and home to live as nomads, albeit prosperous nomads. Why were we willing to part with all that? Because at that stage in our lives, Abram had complete confidence in God's wonderful promises to us. It was a confidence that at times was to be severely tested.

'Leave your native country, your relatives, and your father's family,' God had told him, 'and go to the land that I will show you. I will make you into a great nation. I will bless you and make you famous, and you will be a blessing to others. I will bless those who bless you and curse those who treat you with contempt. All the families on earth will be blessed through you.'[1] 'I will give this land to your descendants.'[2]

God's promises made all the constant upheaval worthwhile, for my one deep sorrow had been our childlessness. I reasoned that there could be no descendants and no great nation without a child, an heir. As we made our way through Canaan, further and further south, my hope—no, my expectation—grew that I would soon be pregnant. In spite of our age being against us, we believed we would have a child. We waited and waited, going through times of danger and conflict, but through it all God protected us and prospered Abraham; he grew in wealth and gained the status of one who could be the father of a nation. But still no heir; doubt started to gnaw at my faith. We made mistakes through the years, but, despite them, the promises from God continued to come to Abram: 'I am giving all this land, as far as you can see, to you and your descendants as a permanent possession.'[3]

Our offspring would be like the dust on the ground, like the stars in the sky—far too many to count.

But although Abram was increasingly respected by the people around us, I saw a despondency grow within him that I could not lift. Somehow I felt responsible for his discouragement: I could not bear him the child he wanted, the child I craved. We had been in Canaan ten years and still there was no baby. It was my failure, my fault.

Slowly but surely, I lost faith and hope; I gave up. My husband was never going to have an heir through me. Yet he still hung on to the promise that he would father a great nation. What was to be done? So I thought of an answer—*my* answer—to the dilemma. The women around us gave their servants to their husbands if they were barren; the servant was the property of the wife and so the baby born from the union belonged to the wife. Quite simple. We *would* have a child, but through Hagar, my servant. Perhaps, as the Lord had prevented me from having a child, this was his intention all along. So I offered my servant to Abram, and such was the longing in his heart for an heir that he took her.

I was totally unprepared for the bitterness of the experience, for the devastation in my soul, as I saw Hagar go to him. When she became pregnant, Abram's joy further pierced my aching heart. I had planned for this; it was what I had wanted, but the baby she carried seemed like *her* child, not mine. Moreover, Hagar knew that she now held a different position within our household, and she taunted me. All respect had gone. Nothing could ever be the same again. What had I done?

In anger I approached Abram, and I confess now that I blamed him: 'This is your fault. You took my servant that I gave you; you made her pregnant and now she despises me. May God judge between us.'

Perhaps Abram felt some shame but he did not take any responsibility. He gave me the choice of what should be done, for Hagar was my servant. So I began to treat her harshly, giving her unending tasks, finding fault at her every step, showing no sympathy for her sickness or her discomfort, ignoring her fatigue. I drove her—until I drove her away. One morning she was just not there. I would have rejoiced openly had it not been for Abram's silence and troubled look. It was for his sake that I accepted Hagar back, for there was no mistaking his relief when we saw her stumbling towards us, exhausted and dishevelled.

From that time on, Hagar was different; she did all I required of her, and I in turn was less demanding. We lived carefully around each other, without conflict but without affection. When her son Ishmael arrived, Abram's joy was bittersweet to me. I had provided him with an heir, but at great personal cost.

Reflection and discussion

- Did any words or phrases in the monologue stand out for you?
- Ur of the Chaldeans was a sophisticated pagan society, but Abram and Sarai kept faithful to God in this culture. How can we remain faithful to God in our culture?
- Abram and Sarai spent some time in Haran before being prompted to move on to Canaan. Frequently God's will for us unfolds in stages. Discuss possible reasons why this is so often the case. Can you give examples from your own life?
- It is likely to have been difficult for Sarai to leave her family and friends and to embrace such a different life-style, even though she and Abram had been promised blessings both for themselves and for others. The desire for

comfort and security can be a barrier to stepping out of our comfort-zone to follow God's plans. Have there been times when you have experienced God's blessing after making a difficult move or stepping out in faith?

- In the monologue, Sarai's confidence in God's promises is gradually eroded by her life experiences. In what ways have you experienced something similar? What helps us to hold on to our faith in difficult times?

- By giving Hagar to Abram, Sarai tried to solve her problems without consulting God. Waiting for God's timing can be a challenge, and the temptation to take matters into our own hands is very real. Share occasions when you have been tempted to do this or have done it. When have you had to wait a long time for God's intervention? In hindsight, were there some benefits in waiting?

- It is reassuring to note that God renewed his promises to Abram in spite of the mistakes that he and Sarai made. Describe times when God has shown his faithfulness and kindness to you, even when you have not been walking in his ways.

- In the monologue, we see Sarai lose faith in God's promises. Is there an element of choice as to whether we hold on to our faith when disillusioned? Think through together how we can hold on to the little hope that remains when we are in very challenging situations.

- Sarai took on the local custom in offering Hagar to Abram, and the consequences were costly for them all. In what ways do we take on the lifestyle patterns that surround us? How can this be harmful? Just because something is socially acceptable, it does not mean that it is wise or the right course of action.

- Sarai, in her anguish, blamed Abram for the outcome of her plan and Hagar's treatment of her. It is perhaps an instinctive human reaction to blame others when the consequences of our choices are tough, rather than admitting the error of our ways, taking responsibility and asking for forgiveness. Sarai's reaction was to attack Abram verbally and Abram's response was to withdraw, leaving Sarai to take the initiative. Neither response was helpful in the situation. 'Attack' and 'withdrawal' are typical responses to conflict. Learning to take personal responsibility and to avoid blaming others may not be easy, but it is important as we grow in Christ. Share your experiences of this process of maturing.
- 'In your anger do not sin' (Ephesians 4:26, NIV). In her frustration and anger, Sarai treated Hagar badly. Discuss ways in which unchecked anger harms both parties. If you are able, share times when you have had anger directed against you or have directed it against others.
- Sarah forfeited her peace by focusing on her doubts and fears rather than on God's promises. Refer back to the prayer at the start of this study. Pray for each other, that you will know God's grace and peace.

Conclusion

Take time to pray through your findings. What might God be saying to you? Is anything particularly relevant to your life at the moment? Write down what you have learnt and refer back to it regularly in the days ahead so that it becomes part of your thinking, reacting and general outlook.

Sarah (Part 2)

Introduction

- Read Genesis 17:15–19; 18:1–15; 21:1–14. You may like to read some of the verses before the monologue and the rest of the verses after it.

- Ask God to speak to you through this episode. You could use the words from Ephesians 3:20–21: 'Now all glory to God, who is able, through his mighty power at work within us, to accomplish infinitely more than we might ask or think. Glory to him in the church and in Christ Jesus through all generations forever and ever! Amen.'

- Sit back, relax and close your eyes. Imagine the scene as someone reads the monologue.

Monologue

Thirteen years went by; the boy, Ishmael, was practically a man and well established in his father's affection. Those were quiet years, settled times, but they were not to last. One day, on God's instruction, Abram altered his name to Abraham, meaning 'father of many'. How he still clung to the promises of God—countless descendants, father of nations, father of kings, the entire land of Canaan! Next, Abraham insisted that he should circumcise himself, Ishmael and all the males within our household. This, God had told him, was a mark of the everlasting covenant between God and those who would descend from Abraham.[4] Abraham changed my name to Sarah, again on God's instruction—Sarah, meaning 'princess'. Princesses give birth to kings, to nations, but I had never given birth. The very name seemed to mock me. Abraham looked as if he was about to tell me more—perhaps, exactly what it was that God had said to him—but, looking troubled, he stopped.

Not long after this, three strangers appeared at our tents. Immediately my husband offered them hospitality: the shade of trees, water and food. At his request, I set about baking bread, and a calf was chosen and prepared. Eventually the men sat under the trees eating and speaking together. I stood just inside the tent entrance, listening.

'Where is Sarah, your wife?' one asked.

'She's in the tent,' I heard Abraham reply.

Another spoke: 'I will return to you next year at this time and she will have a son.'

I laughed inwardly—me, well past the age of producing children; worn out me, to know the pleasure of holding my own child? Abraham was past it too! It was a dream that I had long ago abandoned.

'Why did Sarah laugh? Why did she question whether a woman of her age could have a child?' asked one of the strangers. 'Is anything too hard for the Lord? Next year, I will return and she *will* have a child.'

Who was this who knew my thoughts and reactions? Fear of having doubted the Lord God and of dishonouring my guests flooded through me. I slid further into the tent. 'I didn't laugh,' I lied instinctively.

The one who was the Lord spoke: 'You did laugh.' It was not so much an accusation as a statement of fact.

Later, Abraham told me all that he had held back from me on the day of the circumcisions: how he, too, had laughed when God had told him that I, Sarah, would give him a son and would mother a nation; how he had pleaded with God that his son Ishmael should have the special blessing; how God had reiterated that the covenant was to be fulfilled through *my* son.[5] At that moment, I believed once again that God would keep his promise, and I knew the deep peace born of faith.[6]

So it was that a son was born to us and we named him according to God's instruction—Isaac, meaning 'laughter'. My laughter of incredulity had turned into joyful laughter. God had kept his promise and in our old age I had given my beloved husband a son. After all those years, I knew the wonder of nursing my own flesh and blood, my husband's heir.

My joy was so great that, to start with, I did not take much notice of Ishmael's reaction. Of course, for him, everything had changed. He was no longer to inherit his father's wealth; Isaac would, for he was my son, the son of Abraham's first wife. I suppose Abraham thought that we would all muddle through and that Hagar and Ishmael would come to a point of acceptance.

The day came for Isaac to be weaned and my husband planned a feast to mark this occasion in our son's life. We were in the throes of celebrating, although, as always, I had one eye on my son. He was trying to build up a pile of stones but it kept falling down. I saw Ishmael approach and expected him to help, but he mocked Isaac's attempts. There was no denying the malice in his eyes. Then Ishmael pushed the whole pile over; I had the feeling that it was not the first time such a thing had happened. Shocked, I was about to intervene when I saw Isaac get up and wander off to play elsewhere. I caught and held Ishmael's eyes for a moment and I knew that we were now enemies.

I became lost in my own thoughts—thoughts of fear and panic. If Ishmael would tease Isaac in a public place, what would he do to him in private? Perhaps he had not given up hope of an inheritance alongside Isaac? But it was through *my* son that God's promises would be fulfilled; it was my son who would father the great nation, my son whose descendants would be as numerous as the grains of sand—my son, *my* son. Abraham touched my arm, noticing my silence and distraction.

I turned to him. 'That slave woman and her son have to go.' I was not even able to name them. 'I will not have that boy sharing Isaac's life and and taking any part of his inheritance whatsoever.'

The party was over. I have never seen my husband look so distressed. 'But Ishmael is my son. How can I send him from here?' he said softly.

Abraham walked away and I knew that he had gone to pray. Much later, he returned and told me that he would do as I had requested, for God's promises were for Isaac's descendants. God had assured him that he would take care of Ishmael.

I heard him rise early the next morning and prepare food and drink; heard him speak quietly yet urgently to Hagar and Ishmael; heard Ishmael's remonstrations. But not a word came from Hagar's lips. I watched from the tent entrance as Abraham walked with them to the edge of our encampment, the food and drink now bundled on to Hagar's sagging shoulders. Abraham stood there, staring at them until they were dots on the horizon; then he turned and walked wearily back towards me.

Reflection and discussion

- Did any words or phrases in the monologue stand out for you?
- Thirteen years pass in this story without comment. They were presumably settled times, although, for Sarai, as she was still called, they may also have been years of heartache. Then her life changed completely within the course of a year. Share times when you have experienced sudden change. Have there been times when you, like Sarah, believed that you were 'stuck' in a situation and yet God intervened in ways you would not have imagined possible? How can we live with purpose during periods in which our lives seem to be standing still? In Romans 4:16–22 we read of the importance of faith and hope during such times. Take comfort from the fact that, although Sarah had abandoned her dreams and allowed cynicism to creep in (hence her laughter), God had not abandoned her.
- In the monologue Sarah discovers that the Lord knows her thoughts and attitudes; she lies to save face. In your own time, meditate on the wonderful words of Psalm 139:1–18. David perceives that God watches over us in love, not condemnation. Like Sarah, we are flawed. How does it comfort us to understand that God knows the worst about us and loves us even so? Read Romans 8:31–39 and find time to let these words sink deeply into your being.
- In Genesis 18:14 the Lord says to Abraham, 'Is anything too hard for the Lord? I will return about this time next year, and Sarah will have a son.' What do we believe is too hard for the Lord today, this week or this year? Share your thoughts and pray, remembering Jesus' words in Mark

10:27, 'Humanly speaking, it is impossible. But not with God. Everything is possible with God.'

- We read in Hebrews 11:11, 'By faith Sarah herself received power to conceive, even when she was past the age, since she considered him faithful who had promised' (ESV). It is God's faithfulness that we depend on, not our own. How does this take the pressure off us as we 'try' to have faith? Sarah was commended for her faith; she became the matriarch of the Hebrew people. Read the definition of faith in Hebrews 11:1: 'Faith is the confidence that what we hope for will actually happen; it gives us assurance about things we cannot see.' You may be facing situations that require patient faith. If you are able to do so, share them.

- 'For Abraham will certainly become a great and mighty nation, and all the nations of the earth will be blessed through him' (Genesis 18:18). Sarah and Abraham became the channel through whom God's plan of redemption for the whole world would be fulfilled: through their line, the Messiah would be born (Matthew 1). Read Isaiah 51:1–2 and Romans 4:23–25. Reflect on the enormity of God's plan fulfilled through frail people. How can we take confidence from this, both at a personal level and at a global level?

Conclusion

Take time to pray through your findings. What might God be saying to you? Is anything particularly relevant to your life at the moment? Write down what you have learnt and refer back to it regularly in the days ahead so that it becomes part of your thinking, reacting and general outlook.

Rebekah (Part 1)

Introduction

- Read Genesis 24:1–41 before the monologue and Genesis 24:42–67 after the monologue.

- Ask God to speak to you through this episode. You could use the words from 3 John 2: 'I pray that you may enjoy good health and that all may go well with you, even as you are progressing spiritually' (NIV).

- Sit back, relax and close your eyes. Imagine the scene as someone reads the monologue.

Monologue

We can sometimes look back and recall the one moment that shaped the rest of our lives—one encounter, one decision. And what a small decision mine had been, to offer to bring water for a stranger's camels.

My life-changing moment took place many years ago. I was brought up in north Mesopotamia, over 500 miles from here. We were nearing the end of a routine day and I had gone with my friends to collect water. As we arrived, we were aware of a stranger standing near the well, watching us. I had just filled my jug and placed it on my head to return home when the foreigner came up to me and asked for a drink. Of course, I lifted my jar down and gave him some water. I observed his camels, counting ten in all. They were well laden and looked as if they had been travelling for some time.

'I'll bring up some water for your camels too, until they have had enough to drink,' I offered.

Such a look came over the man's face: pleasure, joy and relief. His gratitude encouraged me on my way as I stepped up and down to the well, drawing water with my heavy jug and carrying it to the watering trough. It was a lengthy job and, by the time I had finished, my friends had long since left. Tired, I returned to the well to fill my jug with water for my family's use. They would be wondering what had kept me. As I climbed up the steps for the final time, the stranger was still there watching me. He approached me once more, but this time he had something in his hands for me: two costly bracelets and a beautiful nose ring.

'Please tell me who you are and whether there is room for me to stay with your family this night,' he asked.

'I am the daughter of Bethuel; my grandparents are Nahor and Milcah. We have room for you and your men, as well as straw and fodder for your camels,' I replied.

Then, to my amazement, the man fell to the ground and started to worship the Lord, the one we, too, served and loved.

'Praise to the God, the God of my master Abraham, for he has shown us yet again his love and faithfulness. He has led me right to the doors of Abraham's brother, Nahor.'

How incredible! I ran home and told my family what had happened, showing them the bracelets on my wrists and the ring. My brother, Laban, immediately gave directions to our servants to prepare the house for the guests and to make space for the camels. He ran to collect Abraham's servant and brought him home, ensuring that the animals and men were well provided for.

Then, most surprisingly, the man refused to eat. First he had to tell Laban his story—how his master had sent him to find a wife for his son, Isaac, from his own family; how an angel would guide and direct him, and how he had arrived at the well after several weeks of travelling and had prayed to God for guidance. He would ask a girl for water and, if she offered also to draw water for his camels, this would be a sign from the Lord that she was to be the wife of his master's son.

Was this not exactly what had happened? Without knowing it, I was the answer to this man's prayer. I stood in total amazement, listening as Abraham's servant explained to my brother and father that the promise he had made to his master was binding, unless my family refused to agree to my returning with him. With bated breath I waited while my brother and father left to discuss the matter. Their answer echoed my heart's desire and response: 'This is so obviously from God, so what can we say? It is not for us to decide "yes" or "no" when God has so clearly shown his will. Take Rebekah with you and may she be the wife of your master's son.'

At their words, once more the man bowed low and worshipped God. Then he gave orders to his companions to bring in precious gifts for my family. I was given silver, gold and beautiful clothes. I had never seen anything as exquisite as those presents.

The feasting and celebration continued late into the night. However, next morning, I was called early by my brother and my mother. They had been discussing arrangements with the servant: apparently he wished to leave straight away. My brother and mother preferred me to remain for a few more days to adjust to the change, to prepare and for us to say our goodbyes. I was to have the final say.

'I'm ready to go now,' I said.

Why was I so sure? I never had a shadow of doubt, never a second thought. Perhaps it was the evidence that God was at work, the excitement and romance of it all, or the impulsiveness of youth. How quick we are to seize an adventure and challenge at that age, to look to the future full of confidence, with barely a glance at the past! I failed to grasp how that parting must have grieved my family.

My mother instructed that my childhood nurse and my maids should accompany me. I would be glad of their familiarity and company as we travelled further and further away from all I had known and loved. As we gathered to leave, my family's blessings and prayers strengthened me. I have always remembered Laban's parting words: 'Our beautiful sister, live in a full and bountiful way. May you have many descendants and may your offspring overcome their enemies.'

The days turned into weeks. As we travelled, there was plenty of time for my excitement to recede, although I remained in a state of nervous anticipation, thinking about the man whom I was to marry. I asked many questions of the servant who had journeyed so far to find me—questions about my new family, their home, their land, and especially questions about Isaac. I came to understand that God had special plans for Isaac and his descendants. The nearer we got and the more the servant told me, the more I grew to love this man who was to be my husband.

At last, the servant informed me that we were nearing his master's home and that the fields surrounding us belonged to Abraham. The afternoon was drawing to a close. Looking up, I saw a man walking towards us across the field ahead. Asking to dismount, I enquired who the man was.

'It is Isaac, my master,' came the reply.

Immediately, my heart beating fast, I pulled my veil over

my face. Isaac approached and spoke at some length with his servant. Then, smiling, he led me into their home. So it was that I was welcomed into their family and became the wife of this man who had inherited great wealth and great promises from God. I cherished the love and tenderness that Isaac showed me as we started our life together. In return, I was able to comfort him as he grieved the loss of his mother; and so we shared our joys and sorrows.

Reflection and discussion

- Did any words or phrases in the monologue stand out for you?
- Rebekah's act of kindness was her life-changing moment. Can you look back and see moments or decisions that completely changed the direction of your life? Share some of them. If you can pinpoint a specific date for your coming to faith, this was surely a life-changing moment. Share your testimony and reflect on the difference it has made to your life.
- Through her act of kindness, Rebekah shaped not only her own future but also the future of a nation. A kind-hearted deed may have a great long-term impact. A biblical picture of this might be the tiny mustard seed, which grows into a tree that can provide for many birds (Luke 13:18–19). How does this picture encourage us in our daily lives?
- We see in this event that both the giver, Rebekah, and the receiver, the servant, received blessing. In Luke 6:38 Jesus says, 'Give, and it will be given to you. A good measure, pressed down, shaken together and running over, will be poured into your lap. For with the measure you use, it will be measured to you' (NIV). Share how an act of kindness

shown to you has made a difference, or how you have been blessed as a 'giver' in a certain situation.

- However, Rebekah did not give in order to receive, but from a genuine desire to meet a need. Neither did she do the bare minimum expected of her in response to the servant's request. Read Matthew 20:26–28. How can we follow Christ's example in having a 'servant-heart'?
- Abraham's servant experienced God's guiding hand in an amazing way. In what ways has God guided you? Guidance takes many forms and may not always be as straightforward as in this episode. You may wish to share areas of your life in which you are seeking guidance and pray for one another.
- The servant received an amazing answer to prayer, and his response was to praise and worship God. Gratitude delights God and benefits us. Read Luke 17:11–19 and Ephesians 5:20. It seems to be a human trait to take things for granted and forget to show gratitude. How can we guard against this?
- In the monologue, Rebekah is seen as decisive and whole-hearted in her willingness to follow God's leading, and several possible reasons are given: ' Perhaps it was the evidence that God was at work, the excitement and romance of it all, or the impulsiveness of youth.' Why can our desire to be wholehearted in following God diminish as we get older?
- Rebekah is blessed by Laban: 'Our beautiful sister, live in a full and bountiful way, may you have many descendants and may your offspring overcome their enemies.' Have you ever spoken words of blessing over someone or been blessed through words spoken over you? One biblical blessing is the prayer at the start of this study; others are

Numbers 6:24–26 (the Aaronic blessing) and 2 Corinthians 13:14 (the Grace).

- Rebekah, by means of her energy and vibrancy, brought comfort and healing to Isaac's grieving heart. We can often help others just by being who we are. Share your experience of this.

Conclusion

Take time to pray through your findings. What might God be saying to you? Is anything particularly relevant to your life at the moment? Write down what you have learnt and refer back to it regularly in the days ahead so that it becomes part of your thinking, reacting and general outlook.

Rebekah (Part 2)

Introduction

- **Read Genesis 25:19–34; 27:1—28:5.** You may like to read some of the verses before the monologue and the rest of the verses after it.

- Ask God to speak to you through this episode. You could use the words from Philippians 1:9–10: 'I pray that your love will overflow more and more, and that you will keep on growing in knowledge and understanding. For I want you to understand what really matters, so that you may live pure and blameless lives until the day of Christ's return.'

- Sit back, relax and close your eyes. Imagine the scene as someone reads the monologue.

Monologue

Isaac loved me, and Isaac prayed for me in my greatest sorrow, my childlessness. Those first 20 years of our married lives could be summed up with those words, 'Isaac loved me, and Isaac prayed for me.' Holding on to God's promises to us through Abraham, we waited, until eventually I knew that I was carrying a child. How I longed for those first signs of life within—the kicking of tiny feet and the punching of tiny hands! They began gently at first, mere flutters, but grew stronger by the day, leaving me in constant discomfort. This baby never seemed to rest. Remembering the wonderful way in which God had guided me to this land, and knowing that the Lord hears and answers prayer, I turned to him in my trouble: 'Lord, you know how I've longed for a child, yet now I am carrying one, I'm in so much pain. What is happening?'

The words of the Lord came to me as they had come to my father-in-law when he was alive—words of promise but words that disturbed me deeply. 'Two nations are in your womb, the two fighting within you. They will be divided: one will over-come the other and the elder of the two will serve the younger.'

When they were born, my firstborn arrived covered in red down, and we called him Esau, 'hairy one'. Our second baby came out clutching the heel of his brother tightly in his fist, so we named him Jacob, or 'heel'.

The twins were so very different from each other, from the start. Esau was always on the move, with a drive that took him far from home to hunt for animals; sometimes he would be gone for several days. Isaac admired Esau's spirit of adven-ture and enjoyed feasting on the meals that resulted from our son's ever-increasing hunting skills. Jacob, on the other hand, stayed among our tents and enjoyed a quiet life. Because of that, I knew Jacob: I understood him. I had time with him and I felt close to him. I carried in my heart the words, 'The elder will serve the younger.'

So my husband and I each had our favourite and our boys knew it. The enmity between them that I had first felt within my womb seemed to grow through the years and, looking back, perhaps we fuelled it. I could see that whereas Esau yearned only to satisfy his physical appetites, Jacob hankered after the double portion that his brother would inherit as the firstborn son—wealth, position, blessings.

One day, Jacob was cooking a lentil stew when I heard Esau returning home. He had been hunting for several days and I knew he would be exhausted and very hungry. I could hear their voices: Esau's was desperate and angry, Jacob's soft but determined. What was going on? I went to look and saw Esau cramming food into his mouth as quickly as he could, stew running down his red beard—and Jacob standing by, looking quietly triumphant. Later Jacob came and whispered to me that Esau had traded his rights as the firstborn son in exchange for the stew; he had sworn it on an oath.

Those words spoken to me by the Lord long ago had begun to come true. My elder son had shown disregard for the blessings of his position, and my younger son had been quick to take advantage. But how would Isaac give his blessing to Jacob? He fully intended to bless Esau as his firstborn: tradition expected it, demanded it.

The years passed and with them came prosperity and, finally, peace with our neighbours. However, there was no peace within our home. Esau had caused us so much grief by marrying local girls who had no regard for our customs and our God; those women made our lives miserable. How could Isaac bestow the promises and blessings that God had given to him through his father Abraham on to Esau, who showed so little respect for the Lord?

Isaac seemed to diminish before our eyes. The strong man who once strode across the fields to meet me was but a memory now. The man before me was weak, bedridden, blind and unable to feed himself. Recognising that his days on earth were numbered, he requested that Esau go hunting and prepare him a meal of game, just as he liked it. Then I heard my husband say, 'I will give you the blessings that belong to the firstborn before I die.'

This couldn't be; I had to act quickly. In no time, I had formed a plan, which I explained to Jacob. He would kill two goats and prepare them to Isaac's tastes; he would then take the meal to Isaac and receive the firstborn's blessing. But Jacob pointed out a major flaw in my plan: Isaac would know he was Jacob because his skin was smooth, so unlike that of his brother. My younger son was afraid of bringing his father's wrath on himself, but I assured him that, if he were recognised, I would take responsibility; I would take the curse. Such was my ambition for him, and my love for him.

As quickly as possible a meal was prepared, for who knew when Esau would succeed in his quest and return? Then I had a stroke of genius, a plan that *had* to convince Isaac that Jacob was Esau. First, Jacob dressed in his brother's clothes, which smelt so strongly of Esau's outdoor life. Then I tied goat skins to Jacob's hands and around his neck. Now he was as hairy as Esau and we were ready to go through with our plan. I passed Jacob the goat stew and my freshly baked bread and sent him to Isaac. I drew as near as I dared and listened. Oh, how many times did my son have to lie to convince his father that he was Esau? Three times...

'I'm Esau, your firstborn son,' he replied in response to Isaac's question, 'Who are you?'

'How did you get the meat so quickly?'

'Because your God gave me quick success in my hunting.'

'You really are my son Esau?'

'Yes, I am.'

There were moments when I thought our game was up, when Isaac seemed to recognise Jacob's voice, but the goat skins on Jacob's hands and the smell of Esau's clothes finally convinced him. Isaac ate and drank while I waited anxiously to hear him bless Jacob, afraid that Esau would come back too soon. Finally, Isaac spoke the words of blessing without which Jacob could not claim the birthright sold to him by Esau so long ago.

'From the dew of heaven and the richness of the earth, may God always give you abundant harvests of grain and bountiful new wine. May many nations become your servants, and may they bow down to you. May you be the master over your brothers, and may your mother's sons bow down to you. All who curse you will be cursed, and all who bless you will be blessed.'[7]

It was done. Jacob had the full rights of the firstborn: we had accomplished all we had set out to do. So why had sorrow and an inner emptiness flooded through me, even as Isaac uttered those longed-for words?

No sooner had Jacob left Isaac than Esau returned. I warned Jacob to make himself scarce for a few hours and I, too, kept my distance. I heard Esau preparing food, entering his father's tent and encouraging Isaac to eat and bless him. I heard the words again from Isaac, 'Who are you?'

'I am your son, your firstborn, Esau.'

Then came the cries of anguish, first from Isaac and then from Esau as they realised the extent of the trickery. There was no taking back the blessings. An enraged Esau ranted, 'Jacob is well called the deceiver[8] for he has deceived me twice: first he took my birthright and now he has taken the blessing that seals it.'

But still he begged for a blessing. There are some things that touch the depths of our beings. When men sob, and when those men are your husband and your son, it is heart-breaking. Isaac had only painful words to give to Esau. What had I done?

Esau's distress turned to seething anger. I watched him

closely, seeing the hatred in his eyes every time he looked at Jacob. Then I heard rumours that Esau was planning to take revenge on his brother once their father had died. Fear gripped me. Once again I needed to take quick action: I had to find a reason for Jacob to depart from us in order to preserve his life. First, I warned Jacob that he needed to prepare himself to leave us, just for a while, to give Esau time to calm down and see reason. Next, I told him that he should take the long journey to my brother Laban's house, and seek refuge there. But how could I persuade Isaac that Jacob should go to live with my family? Then I thought of Isaac's and my past. That was it: we should send Jacob to his own people to look for a wife. Hadn't Isaac been distressed when Esau had married local Hittite women?[9] Somehow I had to play on that, leading Isaac to conclude that Jacob should leave us to find a wife who feared the Lord from among our people, perhaps one of Laban's daughters. So I told Isaac how unbearable my life had become because of the behaviour of Esau's wives, how my life would not be worth living if Jacob repeated his brother's mistakes and married locally.

So it was that Isaac called Jacob to him and sent him on his way with a final blessing—that the Lord Almighty would grant Jacob many descendants and the land promised so long ago to Abraham.

The price I paid was great. Yes, Jacob was safe and the blessings rested on his shoulders, but I was never to see my beloved son again.

Reflection and discussion

■ Did any words or phrases in the monologue stand out for you?

■ Isaac surrounded Rebekah with love and prayer, and in this she was greatly blessed. Are there people who support and pray for you, and people whom you love and pray for diligently? They may be members of your family, but there may be others whom God has placed or will place on your heart to pray for regularly, perhaps over a long period of time. Discuss ways in which you pray for people. Perhaps you use specific prayers or a notebook of prayers and answers; perhaps you pray alone or with a prayer partner or group.

■ Sometimes, what we have longed for turns out to be much harder than we imagined. Rebekah's conception of her sons was in answer to prayer and yet the pregnancy was a painful one, as was the conflict between her boys. Are there times when your prayers have been answered, but the outcome has been challenging?

■ Take some time to pray for families who struggle with their children, particularly those known personally to you. If you are having problems with your children, whatever their age, and feel able to share your difficulties, ask others to pray for you.

■ Rebekah enquired of the Lord, 'Why is this happening to me?' (Genesis 25:22). Wisely, she turned to the Lord in prayer, speaking from her heart. When we face puzzling circumstances, is our first reaction to pray or to turn to others? Rebekah's honesty and sincerity in prayer are echoed by many other biblical characters, reminding us that we can come to the Lord as we are.

- Read Romans 9:10–16, in which Paul reflects on God's words to Rebekah concerning her twins, 'This message shows that God chooses people according to his own purposes; he calls people, but not according to their good or bad works' (vv. 11–12). Now read the parable that Jesus tells in Luke 18:9–14. How are these passages both a challenge and a reassurance?
- Isaac and Rebekah each had a favourite son, and in the monologue this is seen as fuel for the sibling rivalry between Esau and Jacob, causing heartache for the whole family. Favouritism can cause trouble not only in our family life but also in church and community life. Share your experiences of this. How can we guard against it?
- Rebekah's good qualities—her ability to make decisions and willingness to take action—were marred by her manipulative scheming. She felt justified in the action she took, both because of the promise that she had received from God and because Esau had shown such disregard for the Lord's ways. We often fall into the trap of justifying our misdirected thoughts and behaviour, yet God works out his purposes and demonstrates grace. Take a few minutes in silent prayer and reflection, praying that the positive qualities placed in you will be controlled by God's wisdom and used for the good of others and not to manipulate them.
- Rebekah paid a high price for her scheming, as it brought difficult consequences for all those around her, that would continue well into the future. She, too, suffered in that she had to send Jacob away from the family home. This is a stark warning to us that we never act and react in isolation: in our individualistic society we need this reminder. Give examples, whether large or small, of situations you

have experienced or witnessed that demonstrate that we have to live with the consequences of our actions, as do those we love.

■ Refer back to the prayer at the beginning of this study. How has Rebekah's story helped you to grow in 'knowledge and understanding'?

Conclusion

Take time to pray through your findings. What might God be saying to you? Is anything particularly relevant to your life at the moment? Write down what you have learnt and refer back to it regularly in the days ahead so that it becomes part of your thinking, reacting and general outlook.

Rachel and Leah (Part 1)

Introduction

- Read Genesis 29:1–30. You may like to read some of the verses before the monologue and the rest of the verses after it.

- Ask God to speak to you through this episode. You could use the words from Colossians 1:11: 'We also pray that you will be strengthened with all his glorious power so you will have all the endurance and patience you need.'

- Sit back, relax and close your eyes. Imagine the scene as someone reads the monologue.

Monologue

Rachel

The first time I saw Jacob, I was approaching the well with our flock of sheep. He stood among the other shepherds who were waiting for all the flocks to gather. I sensed that they were talking about me.

The first thing I found out about Jacob was that he was immensely strong. As I drew nearer, he walked across to the stone covering the well and pushed it away single-handed: usually more than one shepherd was required to perform that task.

The first job Jacob ever did for me was to water my father's sheep, while I watched in puzzlement. Why was this stranger prepared to help in this way?

The first words he spoke to me, as if reading my thoughts, were, 'I'm your cousin, Jacob—Rebekah's son, your father's nephew.'

He gave me the kiss of family greeting and then broke down and cried as I had never seen a man cry before. What had gone on in his life to cause him such pain and to take him so far away from his family? What sort of journey would leave a man so strong and yet so tender?

I ran to tell my father Laban of Jacob's arrival and he immediately went out to greet his nephew, welcoming him into our home, wanting to know what had brought him to us. Jacob told us everything, saying nothing to defend his actions towards his brother Esau. I loved him for his honesty. He told us that God's blessing was upon him, but there was no hint of boasting. It was clearly God's mercy and goodness, nothing of his own making. I loved him for his humility. My father listened seriously and, when Jacob stopped talking, there was a long silence. Was my father going to send him away?

'You are my own flesh and blood; you can stay here,' he pronounced eventually. In spite of his words, I believe my father *never* quite trusted his nephew.

Those first few weeks of having Jacob around were heady. I felt his gaze on me as I cared for the flocks or moved around the house, and that knowledge thrilled me. I was falling in love, but did he feel the same? After a month my father called me to him. 'Jacob is staying; he has committed himself to work for me for seven years.'

It seemed as if he had more to say, so I smiled and waited. 'The seven years work are instead of a dowry,' my father continued. 'He wishes to marry you.' My delight must have shown in my face, for he examined me closely. 'Of course, it goes without saying that your elder sister must marry during that time,' he said as he walked away.

Seven years can seem like a lifetime to a young girl and a young man in love, but Jacob had an endearing way of telling me that it seemed like only a few days since he had met me. So it was that our love gently blossomed and grew.

But still my parents had been unable to find a husband for my sister.

Leah

The wedding feast was over and it was completely dark as my father led me across to Jacob's house. I had been exquisitely dressed by my maid, Zilpah, in the clothes Rachel had been expecting to wear—adorned with jewels and costly perfume. For the first time in my life I felt beautiful. Yes, I felt I was betraying Rachel; we all knew of her love for Jacob. I knew she was at home at that very moment weeping at the thought of me lying with him; I knew I was breaking her heart. What nobody else knew was that I loved Jacob too.

Of course, he had never looked twice at me. My eyesight was poor, so I moved clumsily and somehow did not really relate to people in the way Rachel could. I couldn't see their facial expressions, so I never knew what others were feeling or how to react. My sister, on the other hand, was altogether lovely. I loved her intensely and felt protective towards her, yet I envied her beauty and natural elegance. But perhaps, just perhaps, I could give Jacob so much pleasure that he would be satisfied with my devotion and loyalty.

'Remember, don't speak,' my father ordered as he left me.

My parents had tried to find me a husband, and every failure had left me hurt and ashamed. 'It is totally unacceptable,' my father had said in private to my mother. 'Rachel cannot marry before Leah; it is just not done.'

Rachel and I knew we had no say in the matter and my mother reluctantly agreed to his plan—to secretly marry *me* to Jacob. It could have been a triumph for me if it hadn't been for the look on Rachel's face. Guiltily I lay in the arms of the man my sister loved, the man who loved her, enjoying his words, his caresses and passion. Inwardly I made excuses, telling myself it was my right to marry first; I had no choice; I would be a good wife. Rachel would find someone else—she was young and beautiful. This was my opportunity. Guiltily I drank in the words intended for my sister, pretending they were for me—deceiving him, deceiving myself.

I shudder when I think of the following morning—the disgust in Jacob's eyes and the accusation in his voice. I sat rocking myself, listening to his fury as he ranted and raged at my father. 'How could you do this? You know how hard I've worked for you. You've known all along how much I love Rachel. Why have you deceived me?'

There was a pause, followed by my father's measured voice, covering up his act of deception with words of reason: 'But you know our customs by now, Jacob. We marry our eldest daughters first. Let's come to an arrangement: finish the week of wedding celebrations and then you shall marry Rachel. I have only one requirement from you: work another seven years for me.'

Jacob agreed, and one week later my sister was also given in marriage to Jacob—one week in which I tried to win his love and failed; one week in which to realise that Jacob would always love Rachel.

Reflection and discussion

- Did any words or phrases in the monologue stand out for you?
- Jacob had encountered God in a very real and personal way during his journey to his uncle. You may like to read Genesis 28:10–22 in your own time. This experience changed him; in the monologue he is described as 'strong yet tender'. We, too, can receive a strong yet tender heart from the Lord. Share if you feel that this has happened in your life. In Ezekiel 11:19–20 we read, 'And I will give them singleness of heart and put a new spirit within them. I will take away their stony, stubborn heart and give them a tender, responsive heart, so they will obey my decrees and regulations. Then they will truly be my people, and I will be their God.'
- In this biblical account we see the beauty of romantic love between Jacob and Rachel, which was given time to blossom into strong devotion. We also see that love comes with responsibility—in Jacob's case, a commitment to work for Laban. Pray for those you know who are starting out in a committed relationship, that their love will blossom into loyalty and devotion and that they will embrace the responsibilities that their love necessitates.
- Leah did not possess Rachel's natural beauty and charms, and in the monologue she is presented as feeling her inferiority acutely. Today, in a society that places so much value on physical appearance and outward success, many people carry a sense of inadequacy. In 1 Samuel 16:7, God says to Samuel, 'The Lord doesn't see things the way you see them. People judge by outward appearance, but the Lord looks at the heart.' Meditate on these wonderful words.

You may like to pause and pray for those known to you who feel unattractive for whatever reason; you may wish to ask for prayer and support if you are struggling with feelings of inferiority.

■ This story is full of deceit: Jacob, who deceived his brother Esau, is now deceived by Laban. We tend to reap what we sow—a principle that occurs throughout the Bible. 'Do not be deceived. God cannot be mocked. A man reaps what he sows' (Galatians 6:7, NIV). Read Proverbs 22:8 and the words of promise in Hosea 10:12. Relate them to verses from the New Testament, such as 2 Corinthians 9:6 and Galatians 6:7–9. In what ways can we sow to reap a 'harvest of blessing' (Galatians 6:9)?

■ In the monologue, both Laban and Leah cover their deception with 'reason'. Our hearts deceive us and we do not necessarily see our hidden sins or motives, tending to make excuses for our behaviour. In Jeremiah 17:9–10 we read, 'The heart is deceitful above all things and beyond cure. Who can understand it? "I the Lord search the heart and examine the mind, to reward each person according to their conduct, according to what their deeds deserve"' (NIV). How aware are we of this self-deception? Refer back to the prayer at the start of this study, praying for the patience and endurance that Jacob and Rachel demonstrated.

Conclusion

Take time to pray through your findings. What might God be saying to you? Is anything particularly relevant to your life at the moment? Write down what you have learnt and refer back to it regularly in the days ahead so that it becomes part of your thinking, reacting and general outlook.

Rachel and Leah (Part 2)

Introduction

- Read Genesis 29:31—30:24. You may like to read some of the verses before the monologue and the rest of the verses after it.

- Ask God to speak to you through this episode. You could use the words from Colossians 1:11b–12: 'May you be filled with joy, always thanking the Father. He has enabled you to share in the inheritance that belongs to his people, who live in the light.'

- Sit back, relax and close your eyes. Imagine the scene as someone reads the monologue.

Monologue

Leah

As we were growing up, there was little rivalry between us: I knew I couldn't compete with Rachel's beauty and she knew I was no threat. All of this changed after we were both married to Jacob; although Rachel knew he loved her, she could not bear the fact that she had to share him with me and that our union had resulted in the arrival of children, whereas her union with Jacob had not. I saw my firstborn son as the Lord's gift to comfort me in my heartache and I named him accordingly: Reuben, 'the Lord has seen my misery'. Then Simeon was born, 'he hears', followed by Levi, 'attached', and I thought perhaps the arrival of my sons would turn the heart of their father towards me and form an emotional bond between us. But my first act of deceit seemed to have killed any possibility that Jacob might become attached to me. He provided for us as husband and father, but I was not loved and he did not delight in my sons as I had hoped he would. No, his delight was in Rachel.

With each birth, the hope of gaining Jacob's affection was renewed, only ro receive another blow, until finally I acknowledged in my heart that it would never be. So painful, letting go of my dreams; so difficult, accepting life as it was and would continue to be. Yet the Lord honoured me with another pregnancy, and this time I did not use my child to try to gain affection. Instead I thanked God for his gift to me and named my son Judah—'praise'.

Rachel

It was our first and only major argument and, looking back, it is not surprising that I angered Jacob. My jealousy of Leah's family and grief at my own barrenness got the better of me, and bitterness started to fill my soul, pushing out the laughter and joy that had been part of my relationship with Jacob. Sleeping with him became the means to becoming pregnant rather than an expression of love. With each period, my frustration and anger grew, until one day I shouted at Jacob, 'If you don't give me a child, I shall die.'

How unfair, when I had only to look at my sister to see that he could father children; how unfair to apportion blame when we were both suffering. His answer stung me though: 'I'm not in the place of God; it isn't me who has kept you from having children.'

45

These were the harshest words I had ever heard from the man who loved me. He would do anything to make me happy—and I mean *anything*. That is why he agreed to give me a child through my maidservant, Bilhah. She bore me two children, born into my lap, claimed as mine and named by me. At last I felt vindicated; I had won the struggle against my sister—or so I saw it. Now I too had given Jacob children: Dan, meaning 'vindication', and Naphtali, 'my struggle'.

However, the animosity between my sister and me only grew. Not wishing to be outdone, Leah gave her maidservant, Zilpah, to Jacob. Zilpah bore him two sons and Leah named them Gad, 'good fortune', and Asher, 'happy'.

The tension between us did not reduce with the passing years, but in the end we learnt to negotiate. One day, Reuben, Leah's eldest son, brought some mandrake plants in from the field. I wanted them, for they were thought to increase fertility. I asked for some but Leah's response was full of resentment: 'You've taken my husband. Isn't that enough? Now you want my son's mandrakes?'

It was true that Jacob rarely asked for Leah at night, whereas his love and desire for me never wavered. So this was my bargain: Leah could have a night with Jacob, in return for the mandrakes.

This arrangement had consequences: still no child for me, but yet another son for Leah. She saw this latest baby as a 'reward' from God in return for her gift of Zilpah to Jacob, and so she named him Issachar. It was a bitter blow, and there was another to come—a sixth son for Leah, named Zebulun, meaning 'honour'. This is what she expected from my Jacob now that she had given him a quiverful of boys. Would she never learn that I had won Jacob's heart and there was no place in it for her?

Oh, it was wonderful to have Gad and Naphtali, and I loved them dearly, but they were not from my womb. For all my pride in them and my outer calm when Leah's daughter, Dinah, was born, I could not move beyond my grief. I lost faith in mandrakes and yet my cry to the Lord for flesh of my flesh rang out day after day.

I could not believe what was happening to me when I started to experience the early signs of pregnancy. It was not until I felt the swelling of my belly and the kicking of limbs within that I knew for sure that God had taken away my disgrace. When my son was born, my cup of joy was full. I named him Joseph, 'may God add', for now that I had one son, surely there would be another. Jacob doted on Joseph; never had I seen him so responsive to a child. There was no doubting that *my* son, Joseph, was his favourite.

Reflection and discussion

- Did any words or phrases in the monologue stand out for you?
- In this monologue we see the pain that resulted from Leah's attempts to earn Jacob's esteem. We cannot force or demand love and approval. In contrast, Jacob and Rachel shared the strong and committed love described between the man and the woman in Song of Songs 8:6–7: 'Place me like a seal over your heart, like a seal on your arm. For love is as strong as death, its jealousy as enduring as the grave. Love flashes like fire, the brightest kind of flame. Many waters cannot quench love, nor can rivers drown it. If a man tried to buy love with all his wealth, his offer would be utterly scorned.' You may have felt, or know those who have experienced, the level of pain and jealousy described

in the story of Rachel and Leah. Pause and pray silently or, if it is appropriate, share your prayers.

- Read 1 Corinthians 13:4–7, 'Love is patient and kind. Love is not jealous or boastful or proud or rude. It does not demand its own way. It is not irritable, and it keeps no record of being wronged. It does not rejoice about injustice but rejoices whenever the truth wins out. Love never gives up, never loses faith, is always hopeful, and endures through every circumstance.' Take time to meditate on this passage and pray that these qualities will be evident in your relationships.

- God saw Leah's suffering and blessed her. God is merciful, sustaining and comforting us. Encourage each other by sharing times when you have found him to be so.

- In the monologue, Leah is seen as letting go of her dreams and accepting life as it is. This transforms her attitude, as can be seen in the choice of name for her fourth son. With the birth of Judah (whose name sounds like the Hebrew word for 'praise'), Leah learnt that it was better to turn to the Lord in praise than to try to win Jacob's approval. Discuss the importance of acceptance and praise in our lives, sharing from your experiences. Refer back to the prayer at the start of this study. Could a change of attitude in an area of your life result in joy as you thank the Lord?

- Rachel's anguish led her to speak unfairly to Jacob. We are warned in the scriptures to guard the tongue: 'Watch your tongue and keep your mouth shut, and you will stay out of trouble' (Proverbs 21:23). Read James 1:19 and 3:3–6, which also speak of the dangers of unwise speech. In contrast, though, carefully spoken words can be deeply healing. We read, 'Kind words are like honey—sweet to the soul and healthy for the body' (Proverbs 16:24) and

'Timely advice is lovely, like golden apples in a silver basket' (25:11). Share times when words have harmed or healed you. Pray together for healing from past hurtful words; ask for self-control, a fruit of the Spirit (Galatians 5:23), and for wise, helpful words in your dealings with others.

Conclusion

Take time to pray through your findings. What might God be saying to you? Is anything particularly relevant to your life at the moment? Write down what you have learnt and refer back to it regularly in the days ahead so that it becomes part of your thinking, reacting and general outlook.

Rachel and Leah (Part 3)

Introduction

- Read Genesis 31:1–7, 14–36, 51–55. You may like to read some of the verses before the monologue and the rest of the verses after it.

- Ask God to speak to you through this episode. You could use the words from 1 Thessalonians 5:23–24: 'Now may the God of peace make you holy in every way, and may your whole spirit and soul and body be kept blameless until our Lord Jesus Christ comes again. God will make this happen, for he who calls you is faithful.'

- Sit back, relax and close your eyes. Imagine the scene as someone reads the monologue.

Monologue

Leah

In spite of the quarrels and strife between us, there was one thing in which Rachel and I were always united—our support for Jacob. From the time of our marriages we had seen our father, at best, take advantage of Jacob's hard work and, at worst, trick him. Our father could see that Jacob was blessed by God in a special way, for our animals thrived and our family's wealth continued to increase.

After Rachel had given birth to Joseph, Jacob spoke more of his homeland, longing to take his sons back to the land that God had promised to his descendants. But our father, Laban, ever the smooth talker, persuaded him to stay and continued to manipulate him, constantly changing their agreements. Nevertheless, once again, Jacob's diligence was rewarded and he grew more and more prosperous: we had huge flocks, many servants, plenty of camels and donkeys. My brothers became angry when they saw Jacob's flocks grow from strength to strength; fearing for their own future, they started to speak against Jacob and influence our father's attitude towards him.

We all sensed the change, so perhaps it should not have come as a surprise when we received a message to say that Jacob would like to speak to us in the privacy of the fields. We went together, Rachel and I, to hear the words that were to send us on the same journey that our aunt, Rebekah, had made many years before. Together we sat and listened to Jacob. He told us of a dream in which God had instructed him to return to his native land, and of God's promises to bless him, for God had seen both Jacob's hard work and Laban's deception. Together we recognised how poorly our father had treated us and acknowledged that the wealth God had given to Jacob was for us and our children. Together we agreed to go; together we packed and prepared our families. Together we left for the land of Canaan, and neither Rachel nor I said goodbye to our father.

Rachel

Why had I taken such a risk? Why had I stolen the household gods from my family? I needed to think quickly: my life would be over if they were found. I could hear my father and his men approaching my tent on their search. In panic, I grabbed the gods and stuffed them under my camel's saddle. I sat down on it just as my father entered. He looked at me with distrust, for had we not deceived him in leaving without saying a word, taking away his grandchildren? I understood that he saw himself as an aggrieved man. Yet we knew that there had been no choice, for our father was quite capable of sending our brothers to remove us from Jacob's home against our wills and force us back to the family home. There could have been fighting, even death. No, it was better to have left secretly.

Perhaps unsurprisingly, our father had followed us, and a week later he caught up with us at Gilead. Jacob was prepared to fight if necessary, but God had spoken to our father, warning him not to harm us. So his accusing words were softened somewhat, for the fear of God was in him. Stealing the family gods, though—that was unforgivable. My husband, not knowing my secret, gave Laban permission to search the tents. Justice demanded punishment, and, being convinced of our innocence, Jacob said that if the gods were found, the person who had stolen them would be put to death.

So why had I done it? Did I really believe that I needed my family's gods, when I had seen the true God bless my husband? Did I yearn for something familiar to take to a strange place—some kind of comfort—or did I want to get my own back on my father, to take away his security? In silence, my father methodically searched my tent. Trembling inwardly, but clear-headed, I spoke: 'I'm sorry, Father, my lord; do not be angry with me. I know I should have stood up to welcome you but I'm feeling so unwell with my period pains.'

He looked at me. In my fear I must have looked drawn and pale—to him, evidence that I was speaking the truth. So he left me, and I remained sitting there, listening to their raised voices. Jacob, deeply offended by my father's accusations, was defending himself. Eventually they came to an agreement and made a covenant. My father's encounter with the living God had changed him: at last he was able to make an honest pact before witnesses; at last he realised that God saw all and judged all; at last there was peace. We ate together and the next day our father kissed us and our children, saying his farewells and blessing us. We were no longer running away: we were free.

Reflection and discussion

- Did any words or phrases in the monologue stand out for you?
- In the monologue, Rachel and Leah are seen as united in their support of Jacob, despite their many differences. In working for a shared objective (the well-being and future of their families), they are able to move beyond their conflict. This is an important model for us, in both private and public life. What are the common goals for your family, your church and community? Perhaps our differences and conflicts become less significant in the light of these aspirations. We are advised, 'A person's wisdom yields patience; it is to one's glory to overlook an offence' (Proverbs 19:11, NIV).
- Rachel, who, over the years, had seen her father tricking Jacob, then acted in a deceitful way herself, taking and hiding the family gods. As children learn so much by example, it is easy for conduct to be repeated through the generations. Share your experiences of this. What behaviour patterns would you like to see being repeated in your family line and which would you like to see halted? The Holy Spirit's transforming work within us has the power

to change and renew us. In what ways have you known this power? Meditate on Paul's words in Romans 12:2, 'Don't copy the behaviour and customs of this world, but let God transform you into a new person by changing the way you think. Then you will learn to know God's will for you, which is good and pleasing and perfect.' Read the encouraging words in 2 Corinthians 3:17–18: 'For the Lord is the Spirit, and wherever the Spirit of the Lord is, there is freedom. So all of us who have had that veil removed can see and reflect the glory of the Lord. And the Lord—who is the Spirit—makes us more and more like him as we are changed into his glorious image.'

■ In the monologue, Rachel examines why she chose to steal the family gods. Although too much introspection is unhelpful, some self-examination before God can lead to better self-knowledge, and is a biblical principle, 'Search me, O God, and know my heart; test me and know my anxious thoughts. Point out anything in me that offends you, and lead me along the path of everlasting life' (Psalm 139:23–24). Do you take time out for quiet reflection and self-examination? How has this benefited you?

■ Perhaps Rachel thought that the family gods would give her security. We, too, can have false securities. Can you give examples? Read Exodus 20:3–5: 'You must not have any other god but me. You must not make for yourself an idol of any kind or an image of anything in the heavens or on the earth or in the sea. You must not bow down to them or worship them, for I, the Lord your God, am a jealous God who will not tolerate your affection for any other gods.' How are the commandments that were given to Moses for the people of Israel applicable to our lives today?

- Laban had a life-changing encounter with God (31:24), which led to a reconciliation with Jacob over a covenant meal. Laban promised to stay away from Jacob, in return for an assurance that his daughters would never be mistreated. In this agreement they found a peaceful solution. Jesus promises in Matthew 5:9, 'God blesses those who work for peace, for they will be called the children of God.' Pray for wisdom and diplomacy for peacemakers throughout the world in the difficult tasks that they perform. We each have a personal responsibility to avoid being the cause of strife wherever possible, and to pursue peace to the extent that we are able: 'Do all that you can to live in peace with everyone' (Romans 12:18). We also read, 'Work at living in peace with everyone, and work at living a holy life' (Hebrews 12:14). This may not always be easy and there may be situations in which confrontation is the right option. Share your experiences of 'peace-keeping' and pray for one another.
- Laban said farewell to his daughters and grandchildren and prayed for them by speaking a blessing over them. We have many goodbyes in life, all of which involve loss: goodbyes to circumstances, relationships and abilities. How can we 'pray' our goodbyes?
- Refer back to the prayer at the start of this study. Like the characters in this narrative, we rely on God's faithfulness to see us through life. Meditate on Lamentations 3:23–24: 'Great is his faithfulness; his mercies begin afresh each morning. I say to myself, "The Lord is my inheritance; therefore, I will hope in him!"'

Conclusion

Take time to pray through your findings. What might God be saying to you? Is anything particularly relevant to your life at the moment? Write down what you have learnt and refer back to it regularly in the days ahead so that it becomes part of your thinking, reacting and general outlook.

Tamar (Part 1)

Introduction

- Read Genesis 38:1–18.

- Ask God to speak to you through this episode. You could use the words of Philippians 1:2: 'May God the Father and the Lord Jesus Christ give you grace and peace.'

- Sit back, relax and close your eyes. Imagine the scene as someone reads the monologue.

Monologue

I live in Egypt in the area of Goshen, the fertile delta area of the Nile. Here my family care for our herds and bring up our children. We have now been in Goshen for 17 years and my twin sons have grown from boys into men. We feel secure here, for we live under the protection of Pharaoh himself. Judah's half-brother, Joseph, works for Pharaoh as the governor of Egypt and this guarantees our safety.

I am awaiting the return of the twins' father, Judah, and his brothers. They are honouring their father Jacob's final request—to be buried alongside his ancestors in the land of Canaan.[10]

When he realised that he was dying, Jacob called his twelve sons to him so that he could bless them and prophesy over them. Judah told me about it afterwards: the blessings that he and Joseph had received had set them apart from the other brothers. Judah's blessing, in particular, contained promises that his descendants would outshine those of all the other brothers. He humbly repeated Jacob's words: 'Judah, your brothers will praise you. You will grasp your enemies by the neck. All your relatives will bow before you... The sceptre will not depart from Judah, nor the ruler's staff from his descendants, until the coming of the one to whom it belongs, the one whom all nations will honour.'[11]

I knew such joy and peace as I looked at our sons that day, such a sense of being blessed. It has not always been so; neither has Judah always been the man he is now.

My marriage to Judah's eldest son, Er, had been arranged by my parents. Judah was not originally from our region, Kezib, although he had settled near us many years ago on account of his friendship with Hirah, a man of high standing in our community, who had come here from the city of Adullam. Judah had taken a wife from among our people, the Canaanites, and together they had three sons: Er, Onan and Shelah.

It was not a happy household to find myself in. Judah was a distant man with a haunted expression in his eyes, and prone to nightmares. He never spoke of his past or his reasons for leaving his family. The household was divided in matters of religion: Judah worshipped the 'living God' of the Hebrews, and his wife had her Canaanite gods. Er was a cruel and selfish husband, so, when he died suddenly, my mourning was superficial. The only genuine tears I shed were because we had no children and I had so little purpose in life. My father-in-law Judah's nightmares became worse after the death of his firstborn; he seemed to believe that Er's death was some kind of judgement from his God. He became harder and even more withdrawn. His primary aim was to continue the line of his firstborn, so a marriage between me and his second son, Onan, was planned.

Any hopes that I held of a happy second marriage were crushed, as was my longing for a child. Onan, while outwardly acquiescing to his father, was also selfish. His was a cunning selfishness rather than an outward rebellion. He feared that I would become pregnant; if that happened, the firstborn's inheritance (which he believed would now be his, on account of his brother's death) would go to my son. The boy would be seen by everyone as Er's child, not Onan's offspring: that was the custom of both Judah's and my mother-in-law's people. So Onan committed a sly cruelty. While seeming to serve his family, he never completed sexual union, spilling his semen at the crucial moment that would have enabled me to conceive a child. I hoped for a change of heart, but it never came: Onan, too, died. Now I, like Judah, believed that God had seen my husband's wickedness and had brought judgement.

Judah was beside himself with grief—and he seemed to fear me, even blame me, for his losses. I had borne no heir and my position in the household was precarious. Judah took the decision to send me home until his third son, Shelah, was older and could marry me—or so he said. I had no choice but to return to my father's household.

Initially I believed Judah's promise, but time dragged on and I became worn down with waiting, with hoping. Shelah was a grown man, and Judah's wife had died; it would have been an ideal time to send for me, but I heard nothing. Finally I understood that Judah had no intention of keeping his word. Yet again I had been wronged by the house of Judah.

When I heard that my father-in-law and his friend, Hirah, were driving their herds to Timnah for the sheep-shearing season, I started to form a plan. Yes, I too could scheme, for

I was determined to find a way to have what was rightfully mine, to give myself a future and hope. I made up my mind to find Judah and remind him of the promise that he had made to me.

So I took off my widow's clothes, replacing them with the garments of a betrothed woman. After all, was I not betrothed to his son, Shelah? This would be my pointed reminder. The veil of betrothal covering my face, I went out to meet Judah at the two springs of Enaim, knowing that he would pass that way to reach Timnah.

Now around Timnah live shrine-prostitutes, servants of our Canaanite goddesses. Sexual intercourse with them is thought to increase the fertility of crops and flocks. Such women have a certain position in our society; they are not regarded as private prostitutes and to lie with one is not regarded as adultery.

There I waited until, at last, I was sure I could see my father-in-law approaching. I stood up to meet him, my anger spurring me on. There was not a flicker of recognition in Judah's eyes as they met mine, but there was something else—lust. He looked me over slowly and I realised that he assumed he was seeing not a veiled betrothed woman, but a veiled cult prostitute.

'Let me sleep with you,' he said huskily.

I saw my chance—my opportunity to gain the upper hand. 'What would you give me as payment to lie with me?' I asked quietly, hoping that he would not identify my voice.

'I will send you a young goat when I return home,' was his reply.

I knew not to expect honesty from Judah. 'I will need to take something from you as a pledge, something that can be returned when I receive the goat,' I insisted.

He was hungry for me. 'What would you like as a pledge?'
'Your seal and cord, and the staff that is in your hand.'

These were given to me without a second thought—was it so easy to be a deceiver? I had all the proof that I would need. So, in the fields by the edge of the road, I had intercourse with my father-in-law in much the same way as I had had with his sons—without love, without passion, without pleasure.

Reflection and discussion

■ Did any words or phrases in the monologue stand out for you?

■ Tamar showed resilience in the face of the difficulties that came her way. How would you define resilience? Some people seem to have more natural resilience than others: they have a physical, mental, emotional and spiritual strength. Are there people whom you admire for their resilience, perhaps those you know personally or those you have read about? It is a quality found in many of the Old Testament women. How can we develop resilience?

■ Judah left his family at about the time when Joseph was being sold to Potiphar (Genesis 37:36). Perhaps he could not face living with his father after playing a major part in the deception (vv. 26–28). Lacking integrity himself, he was unable to bring up sons of honourable character. Although Judah appeared to 'bury' his sin, we see his guilt in his fear; perhaps he saw the death of his two eldest sons as God's judgement on his sin. He was afraid to give Shelah in marriage to Tamar, and once again tried to protect himself by dishonest means, sending Tamar home to her family, having made promises to her that he had no intention of keeping. Judah seemed to be falling further and further away from God's ways. Forgiveness for our wrongdoing, and freedom from guilt, are wonderful gifts, but burying our sin cuts us off from God and takes away our peace of mind. Read Psalm 66:18: 'If I had not confessed the sin in my heart, the Lord would not have listened.' Can you recall actions that have taken you away from God? Could anything be 'blocking' your prayers from being heard by God, or stopping you from having peace of mind?

■ Tamar had few choices in life: her husbands were chosen for her and later she was forced to return to her parents' home. It was a brave step for her to take action to improve her situation, to gain what she believed was her right according to custom. Many girls and women throughout the world still have few choices and opportunities. Pray for those in abusive relationships or who have been forced into marriages, and for young women who have been trafficked. Are there ways in which you could support those trapped by their circumstances and those who dare to fight for the rights of the vulnerable? We are instructed in Proverbs 31:8–9, 'Speak up for those who cannot speak for themselves; ensure justice for those being crushed. Yes, speak up for the poor and helpless, and see that they get justice.' Meditate on the words in Micah 6:8, 'And what does the Lord require of you? To act justly and to love mercy and to walk humbly with your God' (NIV).

■ Tamar took off her widow's clothes (her clothes of mourning) and put on the veil of a betrothed woman, because that is what she considered herself to be. In the Bible, the coming of the kingdom of God in our lives is likened to casting off mourning clothes and putting on garments of praise. Read Isaiah 61:1–3: 'The Spirit of the Sovereign Lord is on me... to comfort all who mourn, and provide for those who grieve in Zion—to bestow on them a crown of beauty instead of ashes, the oil of joy instead of mourning, and a garment of praise instead of a spirit of despair' (NIV). The coming of the kingdom is a cause for joy and celebration. Share ways in which you have found this to be true.

- The story takes an unexpected turn when Judah supposes Tamar to be a shrine-prostitute. The narrator of the biblical account passes no judgement or comment on what takes place next. What can we learn from this?
- Tamar went to meet Judah at the entrance to the village of Enaim, a name that means 'two springs'. Interestingly, the word also means 'eyes'. Tamar and Judah are in the presence of the all-seeing God. We read in Hebrews 4:13, 'Nothing in all creation is hidden from God's sight. Everything is uncovered and laid bare before the eyes of him to whom we must give account' (NIV). Do we have a tendency to be more worried about what others think of us than about what God thinks? Read Matthew 6:1–6. What can we learn from the Lord's teaching in these verses?

Conclusion

Take time to pray through your findings. What might God be saying to you? Is anything particularly relevant to your life at the moment? Write down what you have learnt and refer back to it regularly in the days ahead so that it becomes part of your thinking, reacting and general outlook.

Tamar (Part 2)

Introduction

- Read Genesis 38:18–30. (Other events mentioned in the monologue can be found from Genesis 41:54 to 46:34)

- Ask God to speak to you through this episode. You could use the words from Ephesians 1:18: 'I pray that your hearts will be flooded with light so that you can understand the confident hope he has given to those he called—his holy people who are his rich and glorious inheritance.'

- Sit back, relax and close your eyes. Imagine the scene as someone reads the monologue.

Monologue

My initial plan was to use Judah's possessions to persuade him to give me my entitlement—his son, Shelah. I would bide my time, though; let him search for the shrine-prostitute with his goat; let him realise he had been fooled by a woman; let him worry over the whereabouts of his seal, cord and staff.

However, as the weeks went by, it became clear to me that I was expecting a baby. This was a turn of events that I had not anticipated. I vacillated between fear and hope, grief and joy. I needed to act shrewdly if I was to receive all that was rightfully mine. Meanwhile, I had to wait—wait for Judah to hear that I had behaved immorally and was now pregnant. I expected outrage, for it was a disgrace to his family name. I knew the punishment—death.

Sure enough, in his fury Judah commanded that I should be burned. I awaited the appointed day in terror, and, as soon as the sun had risen, I sent a servant to Judah with the seal, cord and staff. My servant had been rehearsing over and over again with me my carefully chosen words, the words he was to deliver to Judah: 'The man whom these belong to is the man who made Tamar pregnant. Do you recognise them?'

Time dragged by. Why no response? My life and the life of my child hung in the balance, depending on the existence of a small measure of justice and mercy in this man's hard heart. They were qualities I had seen neither in him nor in his sons, yet I could not give up hope. At last the message came: I was called to Judah's house, but there was no promise of reprieve. Petrified, I was brought before him. I was not going to hang my head in shame, though; I would challenge him by looking straight into his eyes.

Judah stood there, his face ashen, and he, too, looked directly into my eyes, 'You are more in the right than me,' he admitted. ' I sent you home and did not keep my promise to give you to Shelah in marriage. I have judged your behaviour and was ready to punish you by death, when it is actually me who deserves punishment, for I have sinned much.'

Judah was a changed man from that day forward. He arranged for me to live securely in his home. I had all the privileges and responsibilities of a wife, except the requirement to sleep with him. Judah never asked that of me again. Six months later I went into labour. The midwife examining me explained, 'You have twins in your womb. I can feel the first arm and hand.' She tied a scarlet thread around the wrist of this baby to mark it as the firstborn, but the babies shifted within me and the other child was born first—a breech delivery. I had two boys—Perez and then Zerah, with the scarlet thread tied around his wrist.

The birth of our sons increased further the respect and kindness that Judah showed me. He wished the boys to be brought up to love and serve the Lord, not the Canaanite gods. At last Judah spoke of his family; together with the boys, I learnt of Judah's lineage, his great-grandfather, grandfather, father and brothers. Finally, Judah decided that we should return to his relatives, and he was reunited with them.

Those early years brought affluence; conditions were good and the livestock thrived in green pastures. But then famine hit Canaan, its severity increasing until we knew that our very survival was threatened. Judah told me that he was going to Egypt with his brothers to get grain, because their father, Jacob, had learnt that food supplies were still plentiful there. All the brothers went except for Benjamin, the son of Jacob's second wife, Rachel. Jacob refused to allow Benjamin to accompany them.[12] At long last I heard mention of Joseph, Benjamin's brother and Jacob's beloved son, presumed dead, in all likelihood attacked by beasts.

There was to be yet more heartache for Jacob: when the brothers returned with grain, Simeon was not among them. The Egyptian governor had considered them to be spies and had demanded to hear their family history. He had insisted that Simeon would be released only if they proved the honesty of their story by returning with Benjamin. In spite of Reuben's entreaties, Jacob refused to allow Benjamin to go.[13] It was Judah who eventually persuaded his father to relent. We were both desperate to get food for Perez and Zerah; they were so under-nourished.

I could see that Jacob's unrelenting grief for Joseph and his fears for Benjamin troubled Judah greatly.[14] 'We cannot go back to Egypt for more food without Benjamin. The governor will not even see us without our youngest brother. Let me take Benjamin,' he begged Jacob, 'or we will all die alongside our little ones. I will take responsibility for him. If anything happens, I will for ever be held accountable.'

We waited for their homecoming with terrible anxiety, but what joy when they returned! Oh, they had so much to tell us. They brought not only grain, but gifts of food, clothes and silver for Jacob, and donkeys pulling wagons. We were all to return to Egypt, to live in security and plenty there, for the famine was expected to continue for several more years. And why was such honour shown to us? The governor had turned out to be none other than their half-brother, Joseph! Judah told me how Joseph had tested their integrity by arranging for a silver cup to be hidden in Benjamin's sack. When the sack was searched, Joseph had ordered that Benjamin be kept as his slave. However, Judah had intervened, telling Joseph that such grief would certainly cause the death of his father. He had begged to become a substitute for Benjamin, for he could not bear to see his father suffer further. Judah had explained to Joseph that he had become a pledge of security and held his father's trust.[15] What must it have cost Judah to ask to replace Benjamin, believing that he would never see Perez and Zerah again?

Joseph had then disclosed his identity to his brothers, assuring them that God was behind all of their circumstances; he believed that God had brought him into Egypt for the very purpose of saving his family. There had been tears and reconciliation.

Jacob's joy filled him with a new lease of life and he resolved to make the long journey to see the son whom he had considered dead.[16] I could see that finally Judah was at peace. We packed up and left our barren land, stopping at Beersheba to make sacrifices to God. Jacob reassured us with God's words of promise, spoken to him in a dream: 'I am God, the God of your father. Do not be afraid to go down to Egypt, for there I will make your family into a great nation. I will go with you down to Egypt, and I will bring you back again.'[17]

Thus we all arrived in Egypt. Jacob sent Judah, in whom he now had great trust, ahead in order to arrange for us to receive directions to Goshen. Here we have lived in peace with Pharaoh's blessing. Egyptians do not mix with lowly shepherds and herdsman, so we are left alone, able to bring up our children to love and serve the God of Abraham, Isaac, Jacob and Judah. Every child we have borne has thrived; every project that we have set our hands to has prospered.[18]

Reflection and discussion

- Did any words or phrases in the monologue stand out for you?
- Read Matthew 7:1–5. Judah was quick to judge Tamar, failing to see the 'log' in his own eye, or perhaps choosing to ignore it. Which do you think it was?
- We are all prone to hypocrisy, whether intentional or unintentional. Jesus likens hypocrisy to 'yeast' in Luke 12:1. Why do you think he draws this analogy? How is hypocrisy dangerous to our spiritual growth? Some Christians end their day with a time of self-examination and prayer. How might this be helpful? Share your experiences.
- Judah's repentance and words of confession were genuine. In the monologue, he is described as 'a changed man'.

Repentance—a deep regret that leads to change—is needed if we are to be truly transformed. In our churches today, are we in danger of neglecting the need for repentance? Read Peter's words in Acts 2:38: 'Each of you must repent of your sins and turn to God, and be baptised in the name of Jesus Christ for the forgiveness of your sins. Then you will receive the gift of the Holy Spirit.' Preceding these words, we read that the people were 'cut to the heart' (v. 37, NIV). There may have been times when we were 'cut to the heart' by our awareness of sin (wrong thoughts, words and deeds, or good left undone). Reflect on the wonderful promises in verse 38. How can we live in ongoing repentance so that the Holy Spirit can work in and through us more fully?

- This narrative is one of great hope. After living contrary to God's ways for so long, Judah's life become exemplary: he won his father's trust, cared for his family and was ready to make an enormous personal sacrifice. God granted him opportunities for reparation. Are there people for whom you hope and pray for transformation? Share your hopes, if you feel able, and pray together.

- Judah and Tamar's story demonstrates God's grace, for out of all Jacob's sons, it was through the line of Judah, and then Perez (who was unexpectedly born ahead of his brother), that the Messiah came. Tamar is named in the lineage of Christ (see Matthew 1:3). God chooses unexpected people; share your experiences of this. Read 1 Corinthians 1:26–29. Why do you think God acts in this way?

- In the biblical narrative, we have information about Judah's past that explains his ongoing sense of guilt, for we read that it was Judah who came up with the plan of selling Joseph to the Ishmaelites (see Genesis 37:23–35). In the monologue, Tamar is assumed not to know all of Judah's history, although she gradually comes to understand parts of it. Often we do not know what lies behind the reactions and behaviour of those we meet, or what has shaped them. How should we behave in view of this incomplete knowledge?

■ Tamar's children, Perez and Zerah, were able to grow up securely in Egypt because of the forgiveness, grace and generosity shown by Joseph to his brothers. Joseph was able to demonstrate such qualities, rising above all that had happened in his past, because he saw the bigger perspective of God at work: 'It was to save lives that God sent me ahead of you… to preserve for you a remnant on earth and to save your lives by a great deliverance. So then, it was not you who sent me here, but God' (Genesis 45:5, 7–8, NIV). Give examples of how seeing something of God's perspective has enabled you to act differently or cope better in a difficult situation. Do you need God's perspective on an aspect of your life now? Share and pray together.

■ Christ is given the title 'the Lion of the tribe of Judah' in Revelation 5:5, echoing Jacob's blessing on Judah (Genesis 49:8–12). As part of that blessing, we find the coming of the Messiah foretold: 'The sceptre will not depart from Judah, nor the ruler's staff from his descendants, until the coming of the one to whom it belongs, the one whom all nations will honour' (v. 10). Here we clearly see God's plan for humanity, stretching through the centuries from Genesis, at the start of the Old Testament, to Revelation, at the end of the New Testament. How does this encourage and strengthen you in your spiritual journey?

Conclusion

Take time to pray through your findings. What might God be saying to you? Is anything particularly relevant to your life at the moment? Write down what you have learnt and refer back to it regularly in the days ahead so that it becomes part of your thinking, reacting and general outlook.

Miriam (Part 1)

Introduction

■ Read Exodus 1:8—2:10. You may like to read the verses in Exodus 1 before the monologue and the verses from Exodus 2 after it.

■ Ask God to speak to you through these episodes. You could use the words from Zechariah's prayer in Luke 1:78–79: 'Because of God's tender mercy, the morning light from heaven is about to break upon us, to give light to those who sit in darkness and in the shadow of death, and to guide us to the path of peace.'

■ Sit back, relax and close your eyes. Imagine the scene as someone reads the monologue.

Monologue

I'm sitting outside the camp; ahead of me are the tents, behind me the lepers.[19] At this moment I don't belong in either group. I have been healed of leprosy, so I am avoiding contact with the lepers. If it were not for God's mercy, I would have been living among them now; I shudder at the thought. But neither am I permitted to enter the camp, for I still have one more day left of my seven days of estrangement. These last six days have given me plenty of time to reflect on my life—the highs and lows, and the failure that caused me to be sent to this lonely place. How difficult it is to be cut off from those we love, from the everyday routines of life, from daily work and purpose! Yet for me, it has only been for six days; for those not so very far from me, many now disfigured and suffering dreadfully, it means a lifetime of exclusion. So I have been looking back through my life, recalling those moments that shaped and changed me.

My parents were God-fearing. I saw little of my father, who was forced to labour for long hours for the Egyptians, so my childhood years with my mother were close. I was quick to sense her concerns and was always hovering to hear her conversations with other women. Times were getting worse for us, the Israelites, for Pharaoh feared our physical strength, born of hard work, and our ever-increasing numbers. First, he demanded that our midwives kill newborn baby boys, but the midwives did not do this, making excuses to Pharaoh. Next, he instructed that our baby boys be drowned in the Nile. By this time, my mother knew she was carrying a child and I sensed her anxiety, as children do, and became anxious myself, longing for a baby sister. When her delivery day came, she whispered the dreaded words, 'It's a boy.'

As soon as my mother saw him, she sensed that he was a special child and told me that we were going to hide the baby. At my age then, hovering between childhood and adulthood, I had enough of the child in me to treat it as a game, but enough of the adult to know that it was a dangerous game. My brother must not be heard; he must not be seen; his needs must be met at the tiniest sound of a cry. I was his constant comfort. A few weeks passed and we enjoyed his first smiles; we watched him getting stronger. However, he was also getting more vocal. We might be able to silence his cries by meeting his every need, but how were we to suppress his gurgles of delight? What would happen when he started to crawl? How were we to hide him?

Then we heard that Pharaoh had ordered house-to-house searches and we knew that we could conceal him no longer. My mother was very quiet after this news reached us. When she eventually spoke, it was to give me an instruction: 'Miriam, go and collect some bulrushes. I need to make a new basket.'

She got to work on it straightaway, teaching me as she went. It was quite a large basket, a miniature version of the Egyptian rush boats that we saw on the Nile. Once it was finished, she said it must be made waterproof with bitumen and pitch. Then she told me her plan. First, we would get our baby used to sleeping in the basket. Then, if we heard that the Egyptians were hunting for Israelite baby boys, we would go down to the river with him in the basket, as if we were going to wash clothes. There we would find a quiet stretch of the river and hide him in his basket in some rushes; it would be well camouflaged. We would be obeying commands: our baby boy would be in the Nile. My mother would return home and I would stay down by the river, keeping an eye on him, pretending to play if anyone came by.

As it turned out, we had to put this plan into action very quickly, and one day I found myself sitting on the bank, watching the basket that held my brother. Then, who should come seeking a quiet place to bathe but Pharaoh's daughter herself? Moreover, she seemed drawn to the very area where we had hidden the basket. I crouched down among the reeds to watch what would happen next. She saw the basket and directed one of her servant to fetch it. As Pharaoh's daughter opened the lid, my brother, seeing the face of a stranger, started to cry. I had edged nearer and nearer, my heart beating, my mouth dry.

'It must be one of the Israelite babies. Isn't he lovely? I must keep him!' I heard her say impulsively to her companions.

Where the words came from, I do not know to this day, but I found myself stepping out from my hiding place and saying, 'I could get you a Hebrew woman to nurse him, if you like.'

She looked curiously at me and then smiled. Did she guess who I was? Could she see a likeness between me and my brother? I will never know, but of course the nurse that I fetched was my mother. Again, Pharaoh's daughter asked no questions, although she looked inquisitively at us both as she said, 'I drew this child out of the water. I want you to nurse him and I will pay you. When he is old enough, you are to bring him to the palace, where I will care for him as my son.'

That is how my baby brother became a prince and gained the name 'Moses', which means 'I drew him out of water'. That early experience taught me much about God's power and protection.

Reflection and discussion

- Did any words or phrases in the monologue stand out for you?
- The monologue starts at the end of Miriam's story. Alone outside the Israelite camp, she has time to reflect on her life. She realises the value of what we so often take for granted: family, friendship, community, daily routines, work and purpose. Have you had times when your circumstances isolated you to some degree? Share what you learnt to value during these experiences. What are the benefits of taking time out to reflect and pray? Jesus teaches us, by his example, the importance of this with-

drawal (Luke 5:16). How do you or could you build such times into your life, either alone or with others?

■ Who are the lepers, the 'outcasts', in today's society? Jesus showed compassion for the excluded people (see, for example, Luke 5:12–15). How can we do the same? At the start of the monologue, Miriam does not belong in either group: she is neither a leper nor fit to be part of the Israelite camp. Many today do not have a sense of belonging. How can we be inclusive?

■ The people of Israel lived through terrible times as slaves in Egypt. Their men were worked to death and their sons were massacred. Yet they also knew a time of great deliverance and joy when Moses led them out of Egypt. On a smaller scale, we experience both dark and joyful times. There is a waxing and waning in our experience, with times of spiritual dryness and times of spiritual plenty. How can it be helpful to us, to know that these changing seasons are only to be expected? Share examples of this waxing and waning from your own lives and the lives of your local church communities.

■ Even as a child, Miriam stood out, demonstrating wisdom and courage. No doubt, her parents' fear of the Lord and her mother's example of faith had contributed to these characteristics. Whose walk of faith has spurred you on in your development? There may be people you have known or people that you have read about.

■ Moses was hidden for his own safety. Many people in our world are in hiding because of their faith, while others have taken great risks themselves in hiding believers. Share examples you have read about and pray together for both the 'hidden' and the 'hiders'.

- Miriam was given the ability to speak wisely to Pharaoh's daughter. We are promised wisdom for situations in which we find ourselves, 'for the Holy Spirit will teach you at that time what needs to be said' (Luke 12:12) and 'If you need wisdom, ask our generous God, and he will give it to you' (James 1:5). Miriam demonstrated initiative and was prepared to take a risk. Share times when you have been given wisdom and the words to say in a situation you have encountered, or when circumstances have called upon you to use initiative and take a risk.

- Help and support came from a most surprising person— Pharaoh's daughter—and in an astonishing way, for Moses was to grow up in Pharaoh's palace. God moves in mysterious ways: share your experiences of this.

- Like Moses, the baby Jesus was delivered from a plan to kill the young Hebrew boys. Joseph was warned in a dream to take Mary and Jesus to safety (see Matthew 2:13–18). Consider in what other ways Moses was a forerunner to Jesus.

- God has a plan for the nations, but the outworking of that plan takes place through individual lives. What does this teach us?

- God had great plans for both Miriam and Moses: from small acorns, great oak trees grow. We read in Isaiah 61:3, 'In their righteousness, they will be like great oaks that the Lord has planted for his own glory.' How does this principle affect our attitudes towards children? What qualities of oak trees would you like to possess?

Conclusion

Take time to pray through your findings. What might God be saying to you? Is anything particularly relevant to your life at the moment? Write down what you have learnt and refer back to it regularly in the days ahead so that it becomes part of your thinking, reacting and general outlook.

Miriam (Part 2)

Introduction

- Read Exodus 15:1–18 and Numbers 12:1–15. You may like to read the verses from Exodus 15 before the monologue and the verses from Numbers 12 after it.

- Ask God to speak to you through these episodes. You could use the words from 1 Thessalonians 3:13: 'May he... make your hearts strong, blameless, and holy as you stand before God our Father when our Lord Jesus comes again with all his holy people. Amen.'

- Sit back, relax and close your eyes. Imagine the scene as someone reads the monologue.

Monologue

The years went by and the Hebrew boy who had grown up in the palace was often a talking point, until one day my brother just disappeared. There were rumours of murder and threats. My brother Aaron and I heard nothing of Moses for years after that; we clung to the hope that he was still alive.

Like our parents, we worshipped the Lord Almighty, God of Abraham and Jacob. The Lord spoke to us clearly, as he had done to our forefathers, so I was not surprised when Aaron told me that the Lord God had given him some instructions.

Nevertheless, I was amazed when he said that he was to go into the wilderness and there he would meet none other than Moses![20] After all this time, would we be reunited?

When Aaron returned with Moses, my joy knew no bounds. They had so much to tell me. Moses was to lead the Israelites from Egypt; Aaron was to be the go-between, for he was known and trusted by the Israelites, while Moses had knowledge of the royal court, as well as the privileges of his princely upbringing, which would gain him an audience with Pharaoh.

However, Pharaoh took some convincing, and the Egyptians, who had oppressed our people for so long, suffered greatly as the Lord Almighty brought down plague upon plague upon them. Finally, Pharaoh said that we could go. Oh, how I remember our departure: the slaughtered lambs; the blood around the door frames; the hurried meal and then the vast crowd of men with their wives, children, flocks and herds pouring out from Egypt like a mighty army. The presence of the Lord was with us in a wonderful way, guiding us and comforting us as a cloud by day and a pillar of fire at night, always ahead of us.[21]

The final escape, the crossing of the Red Sea, is as clear in my mind as if it had happened yesterday. I can remember our fear when we heard that the Egyptians were following us, and our amazement at the parting of the waters by the Lord Almighty. I can still hear the strong east wind that blew all night, pushing back the sea and drying the ground. I can see us walking between the walls of water, and those same waters crashing back on the Egyptians. Such power convinced the people that they should fear the Lord; they believed in him and fully accepted Moses as their leader.

I have never forgotten Moses' words of promise as we stood trapped, the Red Sea ahead and Pharaoh's chariots approaching from behind: 'The Lord himself will fight for you. Just stay calm.'[22]

How we praised our God who had fought for us and rescued us! Moses and I were given a new song to pass on to the generations yet to come, lest we forget God's great works among us. The words flowed from my mouth as I praised God: 'I will sing to the Lord, for he has triumphed gloriously; he has hurled both horse and rider into the sea. The Lord is my strength and my song; he has given me victory. This is my God, and I will praise him—my father's God, and I will exalt him! The Lord is a warrior; Yahweh is his name! … With your unfailing love you lead the people you have redeemed.'[23] Then, to my amazement, words of prophecy poured forth, promises for the people of God, of victory over their enemies and a homecoming: 'You will bring them in and plant them on your own mountain—the place, O Lord, reserved for your own dwelling, the sanctuary, O Lord, that your hands have established. The Lord will reign forever and ever!'[24]

I took my tambourine and more and more women joined me until a huge throng of us were worshipping God, the tambourines beating out the rhythm as we danced in total freedom and joy.

So the three of us guided the people onwards—Moses, their leader; Aaron, their priest; me, their prophetess. There were so many ups and downs in the times to come—miracles, bitter water made sweet, and manna from heaven—as well as terrible times of failure, when the people complained against the Lord.

But my moment of failure was yet to come. Perhaps I should not say 'moment', for the outer failure was the result of ongoing inner murmurings against Moses, and grumblings against God, which I started to voice to Aaron. The truth is that there had already been many moments of failure. Although God spoke to me and Aaron in addition to Moses, it was to Moses that the people looked; it was his leadership they respected, his voice they longed to hear. Frankly, I was becoming increasingly jealous, although I could not perceive it at the time. I suppose we often cannot see the faults in ourselves; we believe that we are justified in our thoughts and reactions. So when Aaron and I complained to each other about Moses' choice of wife—a Cushite—his marriage was just a superficial concern. The real issue was our envy, and, as that festered, we started to voice complaints to others. 'The Lord hasn't just spoken to Moses, has he? He's spoken to us too.'

The words were the outpouring of our hearts, a symptom of the pride within. We lacked humility—the very quality that Moses had in abundance, which fitted him to be the leader of Israel.

The Lord saw our behaviour and heard our words; he drew all three of us to the entrance of the tent of meeting. There, the presence of the Lord came in the form of a cloud, and the Lord called Aaron and me forward into its density. Then we heard his voice: 'I speak to the prophet among you in dreams and visions, but with Moses it is different. He speaks with me directly, not in visions or pictures; he beholds my form. Why are you not afraid to speak against such a man?'

We sensed his anger in every word, but worse than his fury was his absence. Suddenly the cloud was gone and we stood bereft, our hearts longing for his presence, for his blessing. I turned to Aaron for reassurance. However, he was staring at me with panic in his eyes. 'Miriam is covered in leprosy,' he whispered hoarsely.

I looked down at my hands in horror and, sure enough, they were white as snow. Was my body to rot slowly away? Was this to be an outer manifestation of the decay within?

'Moses!' I heard Aaron's voice through my terror. 'Don't punish us; we have acted foolishly. Don't let her be like a still-born baby, with her skin flaking away. Pray for our sister!'

Then Moses, the brother whom I had spoken against, spoke on my behalf, crying out to the Lord, 'Please Lord, I beg of you, heal her.'

I stood rooted to the spot, petrified, staring at my white hands, the skin peeling off them, while Moses remained deep in prayer. But then I watched with growing relief—the relief of a person being rescued from impending death—as my skin started to heal. Joy of joys: I was being restored. We waited in silence for Moses to speak to us. Looking at me he said, 'The Lord has said that you must stay outside the camp for seven days, like other healed lepers, before you can be readmitted. You have caused trouble; just as a daughter who shames her father would have to be punished for seven days, so this must be your punishment.'

So here I am, sitting outside the camp, isolated not just from my family and people but from the presence of God himself. I have had time to repent, time to reflect, time to appreciate what I have and what I had come to take for granted, time to learn humility, time to give thanks for my healing, time to appreciate the gifts of prophecy that God has given me, time to see the foolishness of seeking a status that God did not intend for me, and time to grow in wisdom. How I long to go back to the tent of meeting, to worship, and once again experience the presence of the Lord God Almighty.

Reflection and discussion

- Did any words or phrases in the monologue stand out for you?

- Moses and his siblings were elderly by the time they left Egypt, but God still had purposes for them. We read in Isaiah 46:3–4, 'I have cared for you since you were born. Yes, I carried you before you were born. I will be your God throughout your lifetime—until your hair is white with age. I made you, and I will care for you. I will carry you along and save you.' How can we reflect God's concern and care for the elderly in our communities? From God's perspective, value and purpose do not decrease with age: 'Even in old age they will still produce fruit; they will remain vital and green' (Psalm 92:14). Think of elderly, godly people you know who are filled with the Holy Spirit and maintain a sense of purpose. What do you admire about their lives?

- Moses' early life in the palace prepared him for the task of confronting Pharaoh: he knew the language and understood Egyptian culture. His time in Midian gave him space in which to grow in his relationship with God to such a profound level that God spoke to him 'face to face, as one speaks to a friend' (Exodus 33:11). Miriam, too, had learnt to listen to God and was able to speak out as a prophetess. Aaron had also walked closely with the Lord, so that he was prepared for his priestly responsibilities. Their main spiritual purpose came late in all of their lives. How does this encourage us as we age? God prepares us for the tasks before us, both through our previous experiences and by the power of the Holy Spirit. Read Philippians 4:13: 'For I can do everything through Christ, who gives me strength.'

- Moses encouraged the people, before the miraculous crossing of the Red Sea, with the words, 'The Lord himself will fight for you. Just stay calm' (Exodus 14:14). They were at a moment of crisis when Moses spoke these words: they knew they were being pursued by the Egyptians, and there seemed to be no way of escape. Yet God told them to move on (v. 15). What spiritual wisdom can we learn from these two verses?

- The Holy Spirit inspired Miriam and Moses with words of praise and prophecy in the form of a poetic song. This is perhaps the oldest recorded song in history, passed on orally to future generations. God continues to give gifts through the Holy Spirit: read 1 Corinthians 12:4–11 and Romans 12:6–8. He gives gifts of creativity and of prophecy (such as words, pictures, dreams and visions), as he did to Miriam. He gives gifts of leadership, as he did to Moses, and of service, as he did to Aaron. What is your experience of these gifts, both individually and as a church community?

- What spiritual gifts do you believe you have been given? Pray for the outpouring of the Holy Spirit on you and on those with whom you have fellowship.

- This story shows that God clearly has a plan for women in leadership, as does the story of Deborah (Judges 4—5). Pray for women you know in leadership positions within the church, particularly those under pressure because of their gender. How can you support them?

- Moses, Aaron and Miriam had a team ministry, but God placed Moses in a special position within that team. We read in Micah 6:4, 'I sent Moses to lead you, also Aaron and Miriam' (NIV). Miriam and Aaron were jealous of Moses' position but could find no fault with his leadership, so they focused on the issue of his foreign wife. Is criticism often the result of jealousy? Do we seek to raise our own status by bringing someone else down? Superficial disagreements can cover deeper issues. When we experience envy or feel critical, it is wise for us to go to God in prayer for insight into the underlying issue. If you are able, share examples of times when you discovered that superficial problems were covering up deeper faults. How can we avoid this? How should we deal with legitimate concerns within our families and Christian communities?

◾ Read Numbers 14:27 and Proverbs 16:28. What can we learn from these verses about God's reaction to gossip, complaining, grumbling and arguing? The quality of our speech is seen as a witness to those around us. Why are complaints and gossip so dangerous?

◾ Moses prayed for Miriam's healing, interceding for the very person who had spoken against him. Jesus says in Luke 6:27–28, 'But to you who are willing to listen, I say, love your enemies! Do good to those who hate you. Bless those who curse you. Pray for those who hurt you.' Those who hurt us may be our close friends or even members of our family, as in Moses' case. Are we willing to listen to Jesus' words? If you are able, share your experiences of praying for those who had hurt you. What were the outcomes?

◾ Opposition to Moses, whom God had placed in a position of authority, was opposition to God himself. Read Hebrews 13:7, 17. How are we to treat our leaders? What could we do to support our leaders?

◾ Being put outside the camp was a punishment for insubordination and was also a response to leprosy: by law, lepers had to live outside the camp (Leviticus 13:46). Therefore, Miriam's punishment reflected both these conditions:

her disrespect towards Moses and her brief experience of leprosy. There may be times when we all have to be disciplined by the Lord. Read Hebrews 12:4–13. If you are able, share times when you sensed that you were being disciplined by God. What were the results?

■ 'So also Jesus suffered and died outside the city gates to make his people holy by means of his own blood. So let us go out to him, outside the camp, and bear the disgrace he bore. For this world is not our permanent home; we are looking forward to a home yet to come' (Hebrews 13:12–14). What do you understand by these verses?

Conclusion

Take time to pray through your findings. What might God be saying to you? Is anything particularly relevant to your life at the moment? Write down what you have learnt and refer back to it regularly in the days ahead so that it becomes part of your thinking, reacting and general outlook.

Rahab (Part 1)

Introduction

■ Read Joshua 2:1–24. You may like to read some of the verses before the monologue and the rest of the verses after it.

■ Ask God to speak to you through this episode. You could use the words from 2 Thessalonians 1:11: 'So we keep on praying for you, asking our God to enable you to live a life worthy of his call. May he give you the power to accomplish all the good things your faith prompts you to do.'

■ Sit back, relax and close your eyes. Imagine the scene as someone reads the monologue.

Monologue

We were always on the lookout for spies; in fact, anybody entering Jericho who was not instantly recognised by those at the gate would be followed and reported to the king. The city was in a state of high alert; everyone's nerves were on edge, for we had heard so much about the Israelites—how God had dried up the waters of the Red Sea so that they could escape from Egypt, and how the Amorite kings of the Jordan had been destroyed. Knowing that the Israelite army was just seven miles away, to the west of Jericho, filled us with dread. We were drained of energy, going about our daily lives consumed by fear.

'What could our Canaanite gods do to confront the God of the Israelites, the God of the heavens above and the earth below?' I wondered to myself.

Our consolation was that the River Jordan still lay between us and the Israelites; added to this, our city was fortified with strong double walls, which would be nigh on impossible to penetrate. Moreover, Jericho's position on a plain gave us good vision from every angle: there would be no unexpected attack. Still, we were afraid and, although no one dared to voice such thoughts, I was not alone in believing that their God had promised them our land and that our destruction was imminent.

I guessed who the men were as soon as they entered the inn. My business, set in the walls of the city close to the gate, had thrived over the years. Food, drink and bodily pleasures were available to all at a price. Although I asked no questions, many secrets were disclosed to me. I could see that, from the perspective of the two men, it was an ideal place to come: they found a welcome, nourishment and the opportunity to listen to conversations and ask seemingly innocent questions. They wanted no more, and that in itself confirmed my suspicions: they were spies. No doubt they had been sent here to inspect the city; no doubt the king would already have been told of their arrival. By now his men would be on their way to get them.

Oblivious to their danger, the men finished their meal at a leisurely pace. I knew that I had to act quickly and get them out of the room without causing any suspicion, so I suggested with a smile that they should rest on the roof before continuing their journey. As they followed me, I warned them that we had little time. I was not offering them a place of rest, but a place of safety.

Piled on the roof were bundles of flax that were being dried in order to make linen garments. 'Hide under these and wait until I return,' I instructed them.

A flicker of distrust was in their eyes; why should they have confidence in me? Perhaps they were considering leaving the inn by the way they had entered and making swiftly for the city gates, but a heavy knocking at the door told them that I had spoken the truth and they hurriedly dug their way into the middle of the pile of flax. Content that they were hidden from view, I went slowly downstairs to the door. With a smile and a flutter of the eyelids, I looked from one soldier to the next. My voice dripping with honey, I asked how I could help them.

'Bring out the men who came earlier, for they have come to gather information about our land.'

'Yes, they were here,' I replied, 'but they said little. I had no idea where they came from. When they saw it was beginning to get dark, they left, for they knew they could still get out before the city gates were closed for the night.' My lies came easily: 'It was not long ago—I am sure you will be able to catch up with them, if you go quickly.' I feigned concern, hoping that my suggestion would hurry them on their way. I smiled at the soldier standing at the front and he held my gaze for a long time. Did he believe me?

'I would invite you in, but I know you must be swift to obey the king's orders,' I added.

That was enough: they turned and ran. I went to my window, which was built into the city wall, and remained there until I saw the soldiers disappear in the direction of the Jordan. I watched the last people enter the city as darkness fell; I waited to hear the huge gates being shut. There would be no hustle and bustle on the other side of the walls until daybreak. In my mind a plan was forming—one that could save both the spies and me.

At last I returned to the roof and addressed the pile of flax: 'You can come out now.' What a sight the men were! In spite of the gravity of the situation, I found myself smiling, but as they brushed themselves down, I spoke earnestly. 'I know that you have been given this land. We are afraid because of all we have heard about your God. I believe that your God is the true God: he is the Lord of heaven and earth. You have seen how I have helped you, and I will enable you to escape from here. But promise me, in return for this, that when you take the city, you will spare me and all my family.'

I sensed in these men an integrity that I did not see in the Canaanite men around me. Only men who had proved themselves to be not only brave but also trustworthy would be sent on such a mission. So I believed their promise to me: 'Our lives for yours and those of your loved ones. If you do as you have pledged and say nothing of this, we will protect your family. However, we can only do this if they are all safely in your house.'

'Give me a sign that you will keep your side of this arrangement,' I requested.

One of the men took the scarlet cord from around his waist, saying, 'This is the sign of our agreement. When we have gone, hang this from your window so that we will know where you are. Then you will be protected; we give you our guarantee.'

'My advice is this,' I replied. 'You must go into the hills and hide. Your pursuers won't expect you to have gone in that direction; eventually they will give up their search, assuming that you have crossed the Jordan to safety. If you stay on the plains, you are bound to be spotted. Don't even consider returning to your camp until three days have passed.'

From under the flax I pulled out a length of rope and we fastened it, letting it out of the window. I was grateful for the blackness of the night as they swung down, for I knew that there would be guards on the walls. Pulling up the rope, I strained to watch their departing shadows, but in a moment they were gone. I tied the scarlet cord securely at my window where it was clearly visible, and then I went to rest, satisfied that I was prepared. How long would I have to wait?

Reflection and discussion

- Did any words or phrases in the monologue stand out for you?
- Rahab's heart was drawn to the God of the Hebrews by a deep-seated awe. She was convinced that he was the true God. We read in Proverbs 1:7, 'Fear of the Lord is the foundation of true knowledge.' What do you understand by the phrase 'fear of the Lord'?
- In this monologue Rahab describes how afraid the people of Jericho are, to the extent that they are drained of energy. Fear has a negative impact on our lives, but we may not recognise an underlying anxiety as fear. What fears cause us anxiety and tend to drain our energy? 'Do not be afraid' and 'Fear not' are recurring words in the Bible. It is helpful to remember that these words are often spoken to people who *are* afraid, and that fear is the natural physiological response to threat. Fear itself is not a problem; our difficulties arise when we fail to deal with our fears, and we allow them to overcome us. We can replace fears by speaking words of faith into our hearts: our reason for confidence is

that the Lord is with us. Read the Lord's words to Joshua in Joshua 1:5–9. Discuss practical ways in which you can deal with fear and 'stand on' the promises of God.

■ Rahab demonstrated resourcefulness in hiding the spies and planning their escape. The 'wife of noble character' in Proverbs 31 also has this characteristic (vv. 16–18). Share times when you have needed to be resourceful. God is concerned not only for our spiritual lives but also for what is of practical importance to us. As we apply our God-given resourcefulness, we can pray for the Holy Spirit's help and leading.

■ Rahab lied in order to save the lives of the spies. One of the ten commandments instructs us not to lie (Exodus 20:16), and we read in Proverbs 12:22, 'The Lord detests lying lips, but he delights in those who tell the truth.' However, there have been many occasions in history when lying and bluff have saved lives, resulting in a greater good. How do you reconcile this apparent conflict? Discuss struggles that you may have had in this area.

■ Rahab demonstrated the link between faith and action. Her faith led to risk-taking action, which further strengthened her belief, as we see in her words to the spies. Read James 2:25–26 and Hebrews 11:31, in which Rahab is commended for both her faith and her action. 'Faith without deeds is dead,' says James 2:26 (NIV). How does this challenge us? What actions result directly from our faith? What action could we take as a result of our faith? How much risk have we taken or would be willing to take? Pray for those who put themselves in jeopardy because of their faith.

■ Rahab spoke out about her faith in God to the spies. How does verbalising our faith help us in our spiritual journey?

Take some moments to share where you are in your journey.

■ In the monologue, Rahab is amused by the state of the spies when they emerge from the flax. A moment of lightness can ease a tense situation, and keeping a sense of humour can help us to cope with difficult times. Share your experiences of this. Does God have a sense of humour?

■ Rahab understood that only men with integrity would be sent on such a mission. They had been entrusted with this undertaking because they had proved themselves in earlier situations. We can often see in our own lives that the challenges we have previously faced prepare us for the next task assigned to us by God, or help us withstand a testing situation that comes our way. Share your own such experiences. Read Romans 8:28: 'And we know that God causes everything to work together for the good of those who love God and are called according to his purpose for them.'

■ In many ways, Rahab's faith is surprising. She had heard about the God of the Israelites but, as far as we know, she had not met an Israelite before the spies arrived. We hear of people coming to faith in many ways, some without contact with any other Christians, and some through a direct encounter with the Lord. Encourage each other by sharing any such testimonies that you have heard.

■ Rahab did all that she could and then had to await the outcome. We often find ourselves in similar situations, in which we have limited control over circumstances and simply have to wait and hope. How can we know peace in such circumstances? Read Isaiah 26:3: 'You will keep in perfect peace all who trust in you, all whose thoughts are fixed on you!'

- The scarlet cord at the window was the means of salvation for Rahab and her family, as long as the family members also demonstrated trust by staying in the house with her. In this we see a picture of the scarlet blood of Christ, which brings salvation to all those who trust in him. In your own time, meditate on John 3:13–17 and Revelation 1:5.

Conclusion

Take time to pray through your findings. What might God be saying to you? Is anything particularly relevant to your life at the moment? Write down what you have learnt and refer back to it regularly in the days ahead so that it becomes part of your thinking, reacting and general outlook.

Rahab (Part 2)

Introduction

- Read Joshua 6:1–27. You may like to read some of the verses before the monologue and the rest of the verses after it.

- Ask God to speak to you through this episode. You could use the words from Ephesians 1:19–20: 'I pray that you will understand the incredible greatness of God's power for us who believe him. This is the same mighty power that raised Christ from the dead and seated him in the place of honour at God's right hand in the heavenly realm.'

- Sit back, relax and close your eyes. Imagine the scene as someone reads the monologue.

Monologue

As the days passed by, anxiety mounted in the city. In contrast, I remained silent, valuing my newfound peace and hope. News of the Israelites' activities reached the city: they were on the move and had been camping not far from the banks of the Jordan for the last three days. No doubt they were considering how to cross it.

Then our spies brought news that made us quake in our shoes: the River Jordan had stopped flowing and the Israelites had crossed![25] So their God was working miracles for them again; the courage of many local kings failed.[26] But still the Israelites did not come; days passed during which it was reported that no one had left their camp. The tension in Jericho became palpable. The gates were barred and no one entered or left the city.

At last I saw them approaching, as did all those watching from the walls or from their windows. First the armed guard advanced, followed by seven priests carrying their sacred chest, and finally the rear guard. There were no war cries, just the sound of the priests blowing the trumpets. They marched once around our huge city, far enough away to be out of the range of weapons, near enough for the continual sound of the trumpets to ring in our ears and the pounding of their feet to echo through our heads.

We waited for the attack, but it never came. After they had circled the city, the soldiers returned to their camp, and an eerie silence descended. I had gathered my relatives into my home, telling them merely that I had an 'arrangement' with the Israelites that gave us our only hope of safety. I let them think what they liked about the details of that arrangement. They could see my calm in the midst of the surrounding terror, and that was enough to convince them that, in staying with me, they had nothing to lose and possibly a great deal to gain.

The rumour spread: the Israelites, having inspected Jericho's walls, had discovered them to be impregnable and were no longer going to attack. Nevertheless, our relief was short-lived, for the next day the whole procedure was repeated. Maybe it was going to be a long siege in which they would attempt to starve us into submission.

On the third day, the Israelites encircled us once more, and then again on the fourth, fifth and sixth days. Many people in the city started to relax, their weapons remaining in their homes as they went out to barter for food. On the seventh day, I was woken at dawn by the sound of the trumpets and, looking out of the window, I saw that the Israelites were marching around the city yet again. This time, however, they did not return to the camp but marched round and round—one, two, three, four, five, six, seven times I watched them pass my window. What did it mean? After that, there was a moment of total stillness, absolute quiet, and the silence sent the fear of God through me. Then I heard one man yelling instructions at the top of his voice; this was followed by a fanfare on the priests' trumpets and the deafening noise of all the Israelites shouting, 'God has given us this city!'

There was a rumbling below us, thunder from within the earth itself, then the crash of falling walls and homes. The ground beneath me shook and my home shuddered, but I urged my petrified family, 'Our only hope is to stay here. Don't leave.'

From my vantage point I saw that the Israelites were running towards the fallen walls, clambering over the stones and entering the city. Then Jericho was filled with the terrified screaming of men, women and children and the squealing of animals. Horrified, we had no choice but to listen. For hour after hour it went on, and still our small section of the wall stood; no one entered or left my house. The red cord hung from the window and there I sat until a deathly silence descended. From my window I saw Israelites spattered with blood, carrying items of gold, silver, bronze and iron over the broken walls and away to their camp. My family sat weeping—weeping for all that was lost, weeping with relief that we still lived.

Suddenly, I heard my mother scream and I ran downstairs to see that two men had entered our house. It was the spies. They had returned; they had kept their promise! 'Bring nothing but yourselves,' they instructed. 'This city is cursed and everything in it.'

We hurried out, desperately scrambling through what remained of our city, a city that had fallen into the hands of the living God. As we crossed the ruined walls, we saw that the soldiers had started fires, gathering together bodies of men, women and children, as well as their possessions and dead animals. The stench of burning flesh was overwhelming; I retched.

We were taken to the edge of the Israelite camp and left there for the night. Huddled together in stunned silence, we gazed across at the flames rising high into the sky, and stared at the exhausted Israelite soldiers trailing back into the camp. Too distressed to sleep, we sat watching Jericho being reduced to rubble and ash.

For us, though, there was hope: we were promised security living with the Israelites. Their God became my God; their ways became my ways. It was a new start for me—the opportunity to live a God-fearing life and make good, stable relationships; to marry an Israelite, Salmon, and to have a son, Boaz.

Reflection and discussion

- Did any words or phrases in the monologue stand out for you?
- The monologue describes Rahab as maintaining a sense of peace in spite of the growing anxiety around her. Discuss ways in which our faith acts as 'an anchor for the soul' (Hebrews 6:19) and share times when you have known

peace even though you were surrounded by trouble or pain. Read Philippians 4:6–9. What advice are we given in these verses?

- Rahab's faith protected her family. Share ways in which your faith and prayers have 'covered' those you love.
- The Israelites were instructed to destroy Jericho completely (Joshua 6:17), and the reason is given in Deuteronomy 20:16–18: it is to prevent the Israelites from learning 'abominable' practices that would cause them to sin against God. How can we understand the need for such extreme action? Can you think of times in history when when 'zero tolerance' has been necessary to prevent the spread of evil? What insights do these times give us as we wrestle with the bloodshed in this story?
- The monologue hints at the horror of seeing your friends and neighbours being put to death, and the relief of surviving a massacre. Nowadays, 'survivor guilt' is recognised as a post-traumatic response; for some, it can seem as if they have been 'selected to live' while others have not been so fortunate. Pray for those parts of the world where there is war or where natural disasters have struck. Pray for those who have seen their homes being burnt to rubble and their loved ones killed. Remember in prayer those working with the survivors.
- '"Not by might not by power, but by my Spirit," says the Lord Almighty' (Zechariah 4:6, NIV). The Israelites fought in the Lord's power; there was divine intervention, although human involvement was required. Share your experiences of the truth of this verse. How can we be sure that we are walking by the Spirit and not in our own might and power?

- Rahab was given God's mercy and a new start. She did not earn God's favour by her action, but received it by her faith. Read Ephesians 2:8–10: 'God saved you by his grace when you believed. And you can't take credit for this; it is a gift from God. Salvation is not a reward for the good things we have done, so none of us can boast about it. For we are God's masterpiece. He has created us anew in Christ Jesus, so we can do the good things he planned for us long ago.' Do you have a sense of being God's masterpiece, created to do good things planned by him?

- Read Matthew 1:5. Rahab is one of five women named in the lineage of Christ, three of whom were Gentiles (Tamar, Rahab and Ruth), and three of whose stories involved sexual misconduct (Tamar, Rahab and Bathsheba). All were transformed by God's grace and were given a place in God's plan to bring his Son into the world. Jesus spent time with people like these women, who needed God's redemptive touch in their lives. He was criticised by the religious leaders for mixing with 'sinners' (see Luke 5:29–30, NIV). Jesus replied, 'Healthy people don't need a doctor—sick people do. I have come to call not those who think they are righteous, but those who know they are sinners and need to repent' (vv. 31–32). How are these words both a challenge and an encouragement?

Conclusion

Take time to pray through your findings. What might God be saying to you? Is anything particularly relevant to your life at the moment? Write down what you have learnt and refer back to it regularly in the days ahead so that it becomes part of your thinking, reacting and general outlook.

Naomi

Introduction

■ Read Ruth 1:1–18.

■ Ask God to speak to you through these episodes. You could use the words from Romans 15:5: 'May the God who gives endurance and encouragement give you a spirit of unity among yourselves as you follow Christ Jesus' (NIV 1984).

■ Sit back, relax and close your eyes. Imagine the scene as someone reads the monologue.

Monologue

My friends and neighbours have left me in peace now, here in my home in my beloved Bethlehem. In the quietness I hold Ruth's child, our child, close to me. How my heart filled with laughter when he was born! I marvelled over his beauty and perfection. 'My grandchild,' I whispered.

At that moment my cup was full. As my friends had said, I had so much to praise the Lord for: Boaz, my kinsman-redeemer; Ruth, my dear daughter-in-law, and now this baby boy, who had given me such purpose. He made me feel young again and he secured a future for us all. It was so long since I had known such peace and joy.

My husband, Elimelech, and I knew golden days in Bethlehem, those wonderful years when our two sons, Mahlon and Kilion, had been born and were growing up. Then famine struck and Elimelech decided that we should move east. Of course, I did not want to leave my relatives and friends, to abandon our land, to go away from the place where some, like me, still worshipped the God of Abraham who had led us to this land in the first place—the land supposedly flowing with milk and honey. But then, neither did I want to see my sons die of starvation, so I buried my questions and doubts and we headed north of the Dead Sea, over the River Jordan and into Moab.

My heart never settled there, for my spirit was disturbed. The Moabites worshipped many gods and had idols in their homes; it was all so contrary to the laws of Moses. I clung to my faith and way of worship, while Mahlon and Kilion became increasingly influenced by the culture around us. At least my sons were healthy and strong, and they respected the fact that, within our home, we still worshipped the one true God. At least we were together, and Elimelech and I were able to watch our sons grow to manhood.

Then came a terrible blow: my husband became sick very suddenly and died. My sons were my comfort in those dark and lonely days, through those months when the sense of unreality became a gaping hole. Gradually I dared to hope again for a brighter future. My sons would marry and have families; there would be joy around the corner.

Mahlon and Kilion took Moabite wives. Although this was not forbidden to the Israelites, there had always been tension between Israel and Moab. Nevertheless, Ruth and Orpah were chosen by my sons and were therefore embraced by me. They were beautiful, kind girls and soon won my heart. Ruth, in particular, was interested in our past and our belief in the one God. I was able to share so much of my faith with her. I explained how people were turning their backs on God, doing as they liked and no longer living in obedience to God's ways.

Then cruel tragedy entered our lives as first Mahlon, Ruth's husband, and then Kilion, Orpah's husband, died. They were the blackest days of my life; but for the kindness of Ruth and Orpah, I could not have kept going. We supported each other as best we could, carrying each other through the bad days, comforting each other during wakeful nights.

I wanted to run away from the home that had brought me nothing but sorrow upon sorrow. I could never forget my loved ones—their faces were engraved on my heart—but to leave this place where every nook and cranny, every step and street, held so many memories, *that* I had to do. By then, the famine was over in Canaan and my plans quickly took shape: I would return, albeit destitute, to Bethlehem, to the familiarity of my early life.

With the impetuosity of youth, Ruth and Orpah insisted on coming too. I suppose I was the link to their husbands, our shared grief binding us together. But as we started walking, I realised that I could not let them accompany me. Had not my heart broken many years ago when I had left *my* home-land? I had absolutely nothing to offer them. Even if I married immediately and had more sons, these young women could not be expected to wait for the boys to grow up in order to marry them. No, they should return to their relatives, trust their fathers to find them new husbands, start life again and have families of their own. The girls who had shown me such unselfish kindness needed my consideration. I endeavoured to persuade them: 'You must go back to your mothers. May God bless you and may you find rest in marrying again and having homes to call your own. You have the possibility of hope and a future. This is more bitter for me: my life is over, the Lord's hand has turned against me.'

We wept and kissed. Eventually Orpah agreed to return to her family, but Ruth clung to me. I tried to push her away, encouraging her to catch up with Orpah, although the last thing I wanted was to be left alone. I wondered if I could even survive the journey without help. Yet I had to think of this beautiful young woman. Ruth, though, was determined, and finally her words of promise convinced me: 'Don't urge me to leave you or turn back from you. Where you go, I will go; where you stay, I will stay. Your people will be my people. Your God will be my God. Where you die, I will die and be buried. May the Lord discipline me strongly if I let anything but death separate us.'

Oh Ruth, you saved my life and gave me the tiniest flicker of purpose, for now I had to think of you, help you to become accepted among my people, and teach you more of my God. You were willing to take on my people's customs, traditions and faith; you were prepared to live your life with a heart-broken woman.

Reflection and discussion

- Did any words or phrases in the monologue stand out for you?
- This account, rather like the story of Esther, contains no encounters with God. God appears distant amid the senseless tragedies, and yet he is there, committed to Naomi and Ruth, providing for them every step of the way. If you are able, share times when God has seemed distant. Looking back, how can you see that God was at work?

- Naomi looks back on the 'golden days' in Bethlehem, before the 'land flowing with milk and honey' (Exodus 3:8) dried up as a result of famine. Our tomorrows will not necessarily be brighter than today; we are not promised that they will be. Read Jesus' promises in Matthew 6:30 and 33, and then his teaching in verse 34. However, although treasuring past memories is important, we are instructed not to 'dwell on the past', but rather to focus on the present. The Lord speaks through the prophet Isaiah: 'Forget the former things; do not dwell on the past. See, I am doing a new thing! Now it springs up; do you not perceive it? I am making a way in the wilderness and streams in the wasteland' (43:18–19, NIV). How easy is this for us to do? Share your experiences.
- Life in Moab was 'second best' for Naomi: it was not the place where she would have chosen to be, yet she demonstrated her faith in front of her family. She accepted and loved Mahlon's and Kilion's wives, sharing her life and faith with them. What can you learn from her example to inspire and encourage you if your life has not worked out as you would have hoped? Naomi lived out the instructions given to God's followers many years later: 'love each other' (John 13:34) and 'accept each other' (Romans 15:7).
- Naomi placed the needs of her daughters-in-law ahead of her own needs. She was both grateful and gracious towards them (see Ruth 1:8–9). Orpah's decision to return to her family was reasonable; Ruth's response to Naomi was sacrificial, 'Wherever you go, I will go; wherever you live, I will live. Your people will be my people, and your God will be my God. Wherever you die, I will die, and there I will

be buried' (Ruth 1:16–17). We can hear her sincerity and determination. Do you think that Ruth's words stemmed from love or from duty?

■ We see over and over again in the scriptures that the Lord wants our relationship with him to be built on love, not on duty. We are 'children of God through faith in Christ Jesus' (Galatians 3:26), and Jesus refers to us as friends rather than servants (John 15:14–15, NIV). How can we avoid the dryness of living our Christian lives dutifully? Share your experiences. Our love for God stems from his love for us (1 John 4:19) and the work of the Holy Spirit, who pours his love into our hearts (Romans 5:5).

■ Ruth's loyalty and friendship to Naomi is a great example to us, particularly in an age when commitment is less of a priority for many people. The Bible emphasises the importance of commitment in relationships: in marriage, in family life, to our friends and communities and to our Christian family. In what ways can we protect our relationships?

■ Often, encouragement can make all the difference to us, enabling us to cope with difficult circumstances. Ruth was the encouragement that Naomi so desperately needed. Share encouragements that you have known when going through hard times. Is there anyone to whom you could offer encouragement? How could you do this? Refer back to the prayer at the start of this study. Naomi and Ruth, with God's enabling, endured their tough situation, encouraged one another and experienced a spirit of unity.

Conclusion

Take time to pray through your findings. What might God be saying to you? Is anything particularly relevant to your life at the moment? Write down what you have learnt and refer back to it regularly in the days ahead so that it becomes part of your thinking, reacting and general outlook.

Ruth

Introduction

- Read Ruth 1:16—2:17. You may like to read some of the verses before the monologue and the rest of the verses after it.

- Ask God to speak to you through these episodes. You could use the words from Ephesians 3:16–17: 'I pray that from his glorious, unlimited resources he will empower you with inner strength through his Spirit. Then Christ will make his home in your hearts as you trust in him. Your roots will grow down into God's love and keep you strong.'

- Sit back, relax and close your eyes. Imagine the scene as someone reads the monologue.

Monologue

'Don't urge me to leave you or turn back from you. Where you go, I will go; where you stay, I will stay. Your people will be my people. Your God will be my God. Where you die, I will die and be buried. May the Lord discipline me strongly if I let anything but death separate us.'

It was only as I spoke these words to Naomi that I realised how fervently I meant them. In those hours we had spent together since my marriage to Mahlon, I had come to love

Naomi and admire the sincerity of her way of life. As she told me of her past and of her God, I had been drawn to him, this invisible God. She shared her faith with me, as well as her pain.

My loyalty was with Naomi: her future was to be my future. Had she not welcomed me into her home, shown me love and respect, shared her life with me and comforted me in my grief even when her own heart was broken? I was bound to her by a cord so strong that it overcame our differing ages and cultures—our love for Mahlon and the one true God.

As we eventually neared Bethlehem, thin and exhausted from our difficult journey, we passed through green fields of barley ready to be harvested, through olive groves and vine-yards. There was beauty on every side; I saw now why Naomi called it the land of milk and honey. Entering the town, we could sense that we were being viewed with suspicion, until an elderly woman came forward and, touching Naomi's arm, said softly, 'It's Naomi, isn't it? Could it be you, so altered?' Then others quickly gathered around us with murmurs of recognition.

Naomi's reply was full of anguish: 'Don't call me Naomi; my lot in life has been anything but pleasant. Call me Mara—'bitter'—for the Almighty has made my life bitter. I left you full, but have returned empty. The Lord Almighty has brought me misfortune upon misfortune.'

During our first few days in Bethlehem, we were occupied with creating a simple home, but it was not long before the supplies we had brought with us ran out. We had arrived just as the barley harvest was starting; thank God for that, for his laws gave provision for those in dire need of food. Naomi and I, who had once known security and stability, now eked out a day-to-day existence. The poor and destitute of Israel were permitted to glean—to take the barley stalks dropped by the reapers at the edges or corners of the fields. Naomi reluctantly agreed that I should become a gleaner; it must have been hard for her to endure such poverty in the town where once she had known such respect as Elimelech's wife.

Early next morning, I followed the other gleaners out into the fields surrounding Bethlehem and then stood awkwardly at the edge of one field. It was not long before I was approached by the foreman, who asked, 'You are the Moabitess who has come here with Naomi, aren't you?'

I replied that I was and stammered that I would like to glean in the fields. I asked his permission to follow the reapers. He nodded his agreement and then turned to leave me.

'Who owns these fields?' I called after him. 'Boaz,' was his reply.

We worked all day, taking a short break at midday to shelter from the blistering heat. Oh, it was good to rest my painful back. As the day continued, I would stretch from time to time to ease my aching muscles; on one of these occasions I noticed a well-dressed middle-aged man enter the fields, greeting the harvesters with a blessing: 'The Lord be with you.'

He approached the foreman. 'It must be Boaz,' I whispered to myself. 'So he is a man of faith, like Naomi.' I followed his moves as I worked, saw him deep in conversation with the foreman, noticed them glancing my way, and observed him talking to the other men and women in the field. Then Boaz walked straight towards me. I blushed in confusion.

'Daughter, listen! Stay gleaning in my fields for the whole harvest. Don't go elsewhere: you could be harmed. Note in which field my young women work and follow along behind them. I have instructed the men not to touch you and to allow you to take water from the jars that they have filled whenever you need a drink.'

Overwhelmed by his kindness, I fell at his feet. Bowing low to the ground, I asked, 'Why are you showing me such favour? Why are you bothering with a foreigner?'

His reply brought tears to my eyes. 'You have a reputation here. I've heard about you—how you left your homeland and family to come to a strange land for the sake of your mother-in-law. I've been told of the sadness you have both faced. May the Lord repay you for what you have done for Naomi; may the Lord richly reward you, the God of Israel under whose wings you have taken refuge.'

'You have been so kind to me, even though I am not one of your own workers; you have brought me such comfort,' I responded. 'May I continue to find favour with you.'

Boaz's thoughtfulness continued all day, for when the workers stopped to eat, he offered me bread, wine vinegar and roasted grain, some of which I saved for Naomi. As I returned to my labour, I overheard his instructions to the harvesters: 'Let her glean among the reapers, not just at the edges, and deliberately drop some heads of barley for her.'

A touch of human kindness; a touch of God's kindness. How I longed to return to Naomi and tell her about Boaz! What gratitude filled my heart as I listened to him giving his generous orders!

We stopped as the sun went down and started the task of beating out the grain. I knew joy and satisfaction as we threshed, tired as I was, for I estimated that my first day's work would provide us with food for two weeks.

Reflection and discussion

- Did any words or phrases in the monologue stand out for you?
- Naomi expressed her anguish to the women of Bethlehem. This is a lament rather than a complaint: 'I went away full, but the Lord has brought me home empty' (Ruth 1:21). What is the difference between a lament and a complaint? Even in her lament, Naomi expressed her faith, for the Lord *had* brought her home, albeit empty. There are many laments in the Bible, such as in the Psalms and in the book of Lamentations. Being able to express our grief to God and to others is important. If you are able, share your experiences of this. God wants us to pour out our hearts to him (Psalm 62:8), as Jesus did to his heavenly Father in Gethsemane (see Luke 22:41–44).
- Naomi renamed herself Mara, meaning 'bitter'. Life had certainly dealt her bitter blows and yet she maintained her faith in God and his sovereignty in spite of her suffering. Her faith is demonstrated by the fact that she chose to return to Bethlehem and live among God's people, even though she felt that God had abandoned her. Pray for those who have suffered greatly, that their faith will not die, and that despair, cynicism or bitterness will not defeat them. Pray that those with faith will seek refuge among God's people.
- In choosing to be with God's people, Naomi and Ruth increased their opportunity of experiencing God's grace and provision, which are so often shown through those of God's followers who are willing to be his hands and feet, ready to be generous. Describe times when you have been particularly blessed by being among God's people and

when others have clearly been a channel of God's blessing to you.

■ Naomi shared both her faith and her pain with Ruth. She was honest in expressing her real thoughts: 'Things are far more bitter for me than you, because the Lord himself has raised his fist against me' (1:13). What does her frankness show us? Do we have the tendency to hide what is really going on inside us? Why?

■ Although, no doubt, Naomi and Ruth were relieved to arrive in Bethlehem, they must have been fearful about how they would cope. As Ruth gleaned, however, she discovered that the Lord had gone ahead of her, blessing her, for she found herself working safely in the fields of an upright and generous man. 'We can make our plans, but the Lord determines our steps' (Proverbs 16:9). Share times when you sensed that God had gone ahead of you and prepared the way for you.

■ We read in Proverbs 16:33, 'We may throw the dice, but the Lord determines how they fall.' God was caring for Ruth and Naomi. It was not fate or chance that they arrived in Bethlehem at harvest time, or that Ruth gleaned in Boaz's fields. Boaz, as a descendent of Rahab (a foreigner), would have had a gentler attitude to Ruth than many in Israel who despised the Moabites. It is said that many coincidences in the lives of Christians are actually 'God-incidences'. Encourage each other by describing such moments in your lives.

■ Ruth, in order to receive God's provision, had to show humility by going out to glean. The gleaning laws provided for the destitute (see Leviticus 19:9–10). Perhaps there have been times when you have had to do humbling work, or times when the Lord has taught you humility in other ways. If you are able, share these experiences. Remember the promise in James 4:10, 'Humble yourselves before the Lord, and he will lift you up in honour.'

■ Ruth demonstrated strength of character and diligence as she worked; she showed modesty and gratitude when she spoke to Boaz. We see in this story the importance of good character, for Ruth was already gaining a reputation for her actions in supporting Naomi (2:11). Read Proverbs 3:3–4: 'Never let loyalty and kindness leave you! Tie them around your neck as a reminder. Write them deep within your heart. Then you will find favour with both God and people, and you will earn a good reputation.' What do you think are the outcomes of having a good reputation?

■ Boaz said to Ruth, 'May the Lord, the God of Israel, under whose wings you have come to take refuge, reward you fully for what you have done' (2:12). The picture of being protected under God's wings is a beautiful one and occurs elsewhere in the Bible, such as in Psalm 91:4: 'He will cover you with his feathers. He will shelter you with his wings. His faithful promises are your armour and protection.' Share times when you have known the tenderness of God's care.

■ Boaz went beyond the legal requirements to help Ruth, showing kindness and generosity with no strings attached. Do we worry about having enough or are we able to be generous? Christ promises in Luke 6:35 that when we show grace, treating others well (even our enemies), without expecting repayment, our 'reward from heaven will be very great'. We are to imitate God's compassion (v. 36).

Conclusion

Take time to pray through your findings. What might God be saying to you? Is anything particularly relevant to your life at the moment? Write down what you have learnt and refer back to it regularly in the days ahead so that it becomes part of your thinking, reacting and general outlook.

Naomi and Ruth

Introduction

- Read Ruth 2:18—4:17. You may like to read the verses from Ruth 2 and 3 before the monologue and the verses from Ruth 4 after it.

- Ask God to speak to you through these episodes. You could use the words from Ephesians 3:18–19: 'And may you have the power to understand, as all God's people should, how wide, how long, how high, and how deep his love is. May you experience the love of Christ, though it is too great to understand fully. Then you will be made complete with all the fullness of life and power that comes from God.'

- Sit back, relax and close your eyes. Imagine the scene as someone reads the monologue.

Monologue

Naomi

How anxiously I had paced backwards and forwards that day, asking myself over and over again how I could have allowed Ruth to take such risks. The thought of her being molested, hurt or verbally insulted caused me to shudder and redouble my prayers for her protection. Time passed slowly and, as the sun went down, I went to the door to wait for her. There she was at last, and she was laden, struggling to carry the grain. I rushed to help her inside, longing to ply her with questions, although first she must eat and drink. But it turned out that Ruth had been given plenty to eat and drink; in fact, she had brought *me* food. What a story she recounted!

'Boaz!' I cried out. 'Why, he's a close relative of ours, one of our redeemers. May the Lord bless him who shows such kindness to the living and the dead.'

At that moment, my faith in the Lord's goodness started to reawaken. I, Mara, who had lamented the calamities God had brought upon me, began to trust that God was caring for us and had plans to prosper us.

It was nearing the end of harvest and I had been watching Ruth's admiration for Boaz grow. I could see how much she liked the man, and I couldn't imagine anyone not being attracted to my beautiful, hardworking daughter-in-law. I had also been mulling over her future: what would become of her when I died? I saw it as my responsibility to see that she had a home and was provided for, so I hatched another plan, which I carefully outlined to Ruth as she sat eating at the end of another long day of gleaning.

First she was to wash and perfume herself, putting on her best clothes. Then she was to go down to the threshing floor, east of the village, where the men were making the most of the evening's westerly breeze to winnow the harvest. She was to make sure that Boaz had noticed her while he ate and drank, and then to observe where he went to sleep. Next, when it was dark, she was to lie down at his feet... I faltered.

'And after that?' Ruth asked.

'Then wait... wait for Boaz to become aware of you,' I said softly.

Ruth nodded. She stood up to go and prepare herself; her

fatigue from the day seemed to have disappeared and her cheeks were flushed.

Ruth

Once I was ready, Naomi explained the custom to me in detail: Boaz was our 'kinsman-redeemer': he had the right to take me as his wife in the hope that together we would conceive a child who would continue the line of Elimelech. I was to offer myself in marriage—marriage to this man who had already done so much for us, who had shown me such kindness. His words had lifted me, given me hope that I was accepted as part of this community and accepted by their God. I was not merely accepted by God, but blessed by him who had shown us so much mercy.

So I did all that my mother-in-law asked. My heart beat fast as I lay shivering at Boaz's feet, shaking both from the cold and from my fear, waiting, longing for him to stir, petrified by my own boldness. What was I thinking in taking such a daring step?

Eventually Boaz stirred and woke, sensing my presence. 'Who are you?' he demanded quietly.

'I am your servant, Ruth. Take me under the protection of your wings and demonstrate your willingness to do this by covering me with your garment, for you are my kinsman-redeemer and you have the right to marry me,' I whispered my carefully rehearsed words.

I waited for his response with bated breath; there was a long pause and I feared that I had offended him. After all, why would he want to marry a Moabitess? He was an upright Israelite. But how wrong I was; it was with tenderness and not with anger that he replied, 'You are showing me an even deeper kindness than you showed your mother-in-law. I've noticed your modesty and integrity: you never flirt with the younger men, rich or poor. You are known in the town as having a noble character. Don't fret, my daughter; I wish to do all that you have asked. But there is one person nearer of kin to you than I am. First, I must see whether he wants to redeem you. If he doesn't, I promise before the Lord that I will marry you. Now stay and rest here until morning.'

Rest? How could I rest after hearing such words? Possibly I would be claimed by another man. I realised then that my feelings for Boaz had gone far beyond gratitude and respect: I loved him. My unease grew with each passing hour, and, as the first streak of light appeared, I got to my feet, desperate to get back to Naomi. Boaz sensed my movement; evidently he had not been sleeping either. He warned me to keep quiet about my visit to the threshing floor, while filling my shawl with barley grain as a gift for Naomi. Looking into his eyes, I saw his concern. So he also feared that this could be our parting.

When I arrived home, Naomi was already awake; perhaps she, too, had hardly slept that night. I poured out the grain, and I poured out my heart to her. Naomi put her arms around me and said, 'All we can do, my daughter, is to wait quietly. Boaz won't rest until he has sorted out this matter today.'

Naomi

Time moved slowly that morning, and we barely spoke. Should I have given the girl such high aspirations? Had I, with the best intentions in the world, interfered?

At long last, I heard footsteps outside. It was Boaz. He spoke hurriedly to me, his eyes bright: 'It is done; the transaction is complete. Your nearest kinsman-redeemer wished to redeem Elimelech's land but he did not wish to marry Mahlon's widow, for fear of jeopardising his own estate. The witnesses have given their blessing on our union: Ruth is mine.'

So it was that Ruth, my beloved daughter-in-law, married a man of good character and standing in the community, and our lives were transformed. As for the ache in my heart for Elimelech and for my sons, Mahlon and Kilion, time could never take that away; however, the pain was eased by the knowledge that this beautiful woman was in such loving hands. More than that, my sorrow was lessened by the knowledge that God had never abandoned me: his goodness and mercy had followed me through all the changes in my life, through the valley of the shadow of death and into a pleasant land, a land of milk and honey.

As I held little Obed, Ruth's and Boaz's child, in my arms, I knew that my name should no longer be Mara, 'bitter', but once again Naomi, 'pleasant'.

Reflection and discussion

■ Did any words or phrases in the monologue stand out for you?

■ Naomi and Ruth seemed to see circumstances constantly from each other's perspectives. This was one of the keys to their successful relationship. Consider your close relationships. Are there situations that you currently need to see from another's perspective? If you are able, share these situations and pray for each other.

■ Naomi's and Ruth's shared faith would also have strengthened their relationship. We are bound together by our love for the Lord—like parts of a body, like members of a family, like stones in a building. Which of these similes helps you best to understand the nature of fellowship?

Share times when you have experienced an immediate bond with another believer or been treated as 'family' by others because of your shared love for the Lord.

- In the monologue, Naomi's faith starts to reawaken when she sees God's hand in their affairs. She starts to believe that he has plans to bless and prosper them. Read the Lord's words spoken through the prophet Jeremiah: 'For I know the plans I have for you... plans to prosper you and not to harm you, plans to give you hope and a future.' (Jeremiah 29:11, NIV). Share times when you have seen God's plans working out in your life.

- It would have been important for Naomi to find security for Ruth. In their culture, security for a woman was most likely to be found in an arranged marriage. Naomi could not have approached Boaz herself, hence her plan. Lying at Boaz's feet would have been understood as a willingness on Ruth's part to marry him. Ruth and Naomi were not passive: they looked for opportunities and took those that they were given. It can be hard to know when to be proactive and when to wait. The saying goes, 'God helps those who help themselves'. How far do you think this is true? How can we discern between the times to step out, trusting in the Lord's leading, and the times to 'wait on the Lord'?

- Naomi had to find a balance between being helpful and being interfering. This can be difficult, particularly with adult children. How can we find this balance in our own relationships?

- We are always in a position to pray for the physical, mental and spiritual well-being of our adult loved ones, and for wisdom for them in the decisions that they make. Occasionally, we may, like Naomi, be able to offer advice or help. Pray for each other, for insight into when to speak and when to be silent.

- Naomi eased her own pain by caring for Ruth and, later, Obed. Many people have found that their wounded hearts have been healed to some degree by focusing on the needs of others. Can you give examples of this that you have observed or read about, or from your own experience? We read in Proverbs 11:25, 'Those who refresh others will themselves be refreshed.'

- Taking a step of faith can be risky; certainly Ruth could have lost her reputation, had she been discovered with Boaz on the threshing floor. Our steps of faith may involve risk, although walking closely with the Lord reduces the likelihood of going off course. We have the comforting promise, 'Whether you turn to the right or the left, your ears will hear a voice behind you, saying, "This is the way; walk in it"' (Isaiah 30:21, NIV). Describe risky steps of faith you have taken, or times when you have gone off track. What were the outcomes?

- For Ruth, the situation did not immediately work out as she had hoped, for there was a closer relative than Boaz who had to be consulted. She had to trust God and wait. Pray together for any situations that you have entrusted to God. Perhaps, like Ruth, you have taken action and are now waiting for the outcome.

- At the end of the monologue, we leave Naomi caring for her grandson Obed, confident in the knowledge that God's goodness and mercy has followed her all the days of her life (see Psalm 23). She has renewed hope and purpose. Share times when changed circumstances have given you a new optimism.

- We find Ruth, a foreigner, like Rahab, in the lineage of David and Jesus (Matthew 1:5–6). Far more blessing than she could ever have imagined came from her union with Boaz. Are there times when God's blessings in your life have had far-reaching effects?
- Boaz was Naomi's and Ruth's kinsman-redeemer, a relative who voluntarily took responsibility for the extended family of a dead man, showing them favour and giving them a secure future. The kinsman-redeemer is a picture of Christ; through his death and resurrection we are brought into a position of favour with God, our lives are redeemed, and we are given a secure future. Share your experiences of finding this security.

Conclusion

Take time to pray through your findings. What might God be saying to you? Is anything particularly relevant to your life at the moment? Write down what you have learnt and refer back to it regularly in the days ahead so that it becomes part of your thinking, reacting and general outlook.

Hannah

Introduction

- Read 1 Samuel 1:1—2:11, 18–21. You may like to read 1 Samuel 1 before the monologue and the verses from 1 Samuel 2 after the monologue.

- Ask God to speak to you through these episodes. You could use the words from Luke 1:46–49: 'Oh, how my soul praises the Lord. How my spirit rejoices in God my Saviour! For he took notice of his lowly servant girl, and from now on all generations will call me blessed. For the Mighty One is holy, and has done great things for me.'

- Sit back, relax and close your eyes. Imagine the scene as someone reads the monologue.

Monologue

When we were first married, the yearly trip to Shiloh was such a joy for me, but I had grown to dread it, for it was a reminder of the passing of time and my unmet longings. I had no children, and my husband, although he loved me dearly, had taken a second wife who had produced not just one child for him, but several. Peninnah, their mother, spent her days admiring her developing offspring.

There was one thing *I* had, though, that she resented deeply—the love of our husband. Elkanah was everything a husband should be to Peninnah, but I knew, and she knew, that I held his heart. So, rather than me being envious of Peninnah, she was bitterly jealous of me. She showed her feelings in a most cruel way, taunting me with her sly looks as she discussed her children with Elkanah. As their family grew, I felt pushed out more and more into the shadows. My husband could never understand why his love for me was not sufficient to assuage the yearnings of my heart, and this caused him sorrow; my guilt over this only added to my suffering.

Elkanah was successful in his business and we prospered. He was a godly man and took seriously our annual visit to Shiloh, where we worshipped and sacrificed as a family. According to custom, he would give the priests their share of our sacrifice and then give Peninnah and each of her children a portion of the meat. Sensing my anguish, he would give me a double portion. This only served to fuel Peninnah's jealousy further, and, as she laughed, sang and played with her children, she would deliberately and cunningly exclude me. In my misery, I could not join in the celebrations that followed the sacrifice. Unable to eat or drink, I would break into uncontrollable weeping. Elkanah tried to comfort me but in vain, for he could not answer my most pressing question. Why had the Lord closed my womb?

Finally, one year, I could bear it no longer. There was only one place where I could go in the hope of comfort and that was to God's dwelling place. After everyone else had feasted, I rose silently and went to the house of the Lord, passing Eli the priest who was sitting at the entrance. Once inside, I fell on my knees and poured out my heart to the Lord.

So deep was my distress that I made a promise, one that was to cost me dearly to keep: 'Lord Almighty, if you will look on me, your servant, and see my sorrow and pain, if you will give me a son, then I will give him to you for the rest of his life. I will fulfil the Nazarite vows and no razor shall ever touch his head.'

The words came silently from my lips. So lost was I in my pleas that I had not heard Eli enter and approach me. His angry voice cut through my prayer, asking me how long I intended to continue in this unseemly behaviour—so clearly feeling the after-effects of feasting and drinking. I was horrified that he thought I was drunk, and perhaps it was this that enabled me to find my voice.

'I have not had too much wine, my lord. In fact, I have not touched a drop. Do not take me for a wicked woman. I have been pouring my troubled soul out before the Lord; I have been telling him of my anguish.'

Eli's anger melted and I saw in his eyes that he, too, knew great sadness. 'Go in peace,' he replied, 'and may the God of Israel give you what you have requested.'

He didn't ask me what my prayer had been; he simply trusted that God could do all that I had asked of him.

'May I be worthy of your approval,' I responded as I stood to leave the place of worship.

With every step towards Elkanah, my wretchedness diminished, and, by the time I had rejoined the party, joy had flooded through me. Suddenly I felt hungry and, much to Elkanah's delight, found myself entering into the celebrations and feasting. Early the next day we worshipped the Lord together and then returned to Ramah, a renewed hope burning within me.

It was not long before I conceived and bore a son, calling him Samuel, which means 'offspring of God', for I had asked the Lord for him. That little child was my delight.

I spoke to Elkanah of my conversation with Eli the priest

and of my promise to God. Being a righteous man, he understood that I must carry out my promise—but not just yet. I would stay for a few years at home with my child; I would not go again to Shiloh until Samuel was weaned. So I would watch Elkanah, Peninnah, the children and some of the servants set off to offer their sacrifices each year.

How I savoured those quiet times with my son, preparing him for what lay ahead. As soon as I felt that Samuel was able to understand, I would tell him of our plans to take him to help Eli at Shiloh, explaining that he would be in the presence of the Lord and serve him there for ever. As I spoke, Samuel would gaze into my eyes with complete trust and acceptance. I would assure him of my love—that wherever he was and wherever I was, he would hold a special place in my heart and would always be in my thoughts and prayers.

Then came the day when Samuel was fully weaned and I knew that my time with my son was drawing to a close. How quickly it had passed! I feared the pain of our separation, both for him and for me. Who would embrace him and comfort him? Who would nurse him when he was sick? Who would listen to him and laugh with him?

When the next visit to Shiloh approached, I prepared to go with Elkanah. All too soon the sacrifices were made; all too soon came the time to take our child to Eli.

'My lord.' I spoke huskily, my throat constricted with emotion. 'I am the woman who was standing here once in your presence praying to the Lord. It is this child that I prayed for; the Lord responded to my plea. Now I offer him to God: as long as Samuel lives, I give him to the Lord.' Eli praised and worshipped God.

As I gave my most precious gift to the Lord, a song sprang up in my heart, a song that gave me strength even in the sorrow of parting: 'My heart rejoices in the Lord! The Lord has made me strong. Now I have an answer for my enemies; I rejoice because you rescued me. No one is holy like the Lord! There is no one besides you; there is no Rock like our God.'[27]

Each year, I poured my love for Samuel into making a robe for him, which I would give him when we went to Shiloh to worship. Eli was pleased with his progress; Samuel was clearly a blessing to the priest. We saw that Samuel was growing in godliness and in the ministry given to him. We noticed how well loved he was by those who came to worship, and we were comforted.

Before returning home each year, Elkanah and I received a blessing from Eli: he prayed that God would give us children to take the place of Samuel, who had been dedicated to God. How the Lord blessed us over the years, for we had three more sons and two daughters.

Reflection and discussion

- Did any words or phrases in the monologue stand out for you?
- Although polygamy was not God's intention for his people (Genesis 2:24), it had become an accepted custom among the Israelites. One of the reasons for this was the importance of providing offspring to help the father in his work, to care for elderly parents and to ensure the continuation of the family line. Elkanah could have divorced Hannah for her barrenness, but instead he remained in a loving relationship with her. However, the situation in the household resulted in friction. This appears to have been of Peninnah's making, for she envied the relationship between Elkanah and Hannah and retaliated by taunting

Hannah about her childlessness. One of the ten commandments instructs us not to covet what others have (Exodus 20:17). Read 1 Timothy 6:6–8 and James 3:15–18. In what ways is envy destructive to us, physically, emotionally and spiritually? In which areas of our lives are we most likely to become envious? How can we foster contentment?

■ Hannah did not retaliate, although she was deeply grieved by Peninnah's behaviour. Perhaps she knew the teaching of Leviticus 19:17–18: 'Do not nurse hatred in your heart for any of your relatives... Do not seek revenge or bear a grudge... but love your neighbour as yourself.' This command was repeated by Jesus: '"Love the Lord your God with all your heart and with all your soul and with all your mind." This is the first and greatest commandment. And the second is like it: "Love your neighbour as yourself." All the Law and the Prophets hang on these two commandments' (Matthew 22:37–40, NIV). How does obedience to the first of these commandments enable us to obey the second? If you feel able, share relationships in which you are finding it hard to live at peace. Support and pray for each other.

■ In the monologue, Hannah recognises that no human being can comfort her fully. Clearly she is at the end of her own resources; she cannot even eat. It is at this point that we see her approaching the house of God and coming into his presence. Perhaps you can recall times when, at the end of your tether, you have turned to the Lord. Hannah told Eli that she had been pouring out her soul before the Lord. This practice is found elsewhere in scripture, notably in the Psalms. It is something that we are instructed to do: 'Cast your cares on the Lord and he will sustain you' (Psalm 55:22, NIV). Meditate on this and the following verses: 'Pour out your heart like water before the presence of the Lord!' (Lamentations 2:19, ESV). 'Give all your worries and cares to God, for he cares about you' (1 Peter 5:7). Share occasions when you have done this. What were the outcomes?

- Hannah was able to voice both her indignation and her true predicament when Eli accused her of being drunk. This must have been difficult, given the stress that she was under and who she was speaking to. God wants to give us the courage to speak out when the need arises. We are his voice, as well as his hands and feet. What might God be wanting you to speak out about?

- Hannah kept her promise to give Samuel to the Lord, however hard this must have been for her. Do you know people who have made painful sacrifices in living their lives for God? Share some examples. They may be people you have known personally or those you have read about. Where appropriate, pray for them.

- This story speaks to us of stewardship: everything we have is lent to us by God. How does this affect the way we treat the people and possessions in our lives? How can we hold on lightly to what we have? How does this give us freedom?

- Eli prayed for two things for Hannah: that she should know peace and that God would answer the cries of her heart. One of these prayers was answered immediately, for Hannah went away in a completely different frame of mind: 'she was no longer sad' (1 Samuel 1:18). The other prayer was answered 'in due time' (v. 20). What can we learn from the fact that Eli neither asked probing questions nor tried to provide all the answers? Share times when you have been lifted by another's prayers for you.

If you are currently in need, is there someone you could approach for prayer support, even if you are not in a position to share the details of your situation?

■ Eli's sensitivity was shown again when Hannah returned with Elkanah in the years to come. He appreciated the cost to her of giving up Samuel, and continued to pray for the couple, that they would be blessed with more children. Are there situations or people that have been placed in your path that you can continue to hold in your prayers? A few words or a short prayer can make all the difference to someone's day.

■ Hannah's song of praise shows us that she experienced joy as a result of obeying God, even though she suffered because she was parted from her son. Her song shows us the extent of the inward journey that Hannah took, for she learnt to rejoice in the Lord who had made her strong (2:1–2), in spite of her heartache. Share times when you have experienced joy after taking a step of costly obedience.

■ Hannah's song connects to other songs of praise sung by women in the Bible, notably Mary's song in Luke 1:46–55, from which the prayer at the start of this study came. The prophetic ending to Hannah's song makes a reference to the 'anointed one' to come, the Messiah. In your own time you might like to write your own song of praise.

Conclusion

Take time to pray through your findings. What might God be saying to you? Is anything particularly relevant to your life at the moment? Write down what you have learnt and refer back to it regularly in the days ahead so that it becomes part of your thinking, reacting and general outlook.

Bathsheba (Part 1)

Introduction

- Read 2 Samuel 11; 12:13–24a. You may like to read some of the verses before the monologue and the rest of the verses after it.

- Ask God to speak to you through this episode. You could use David's words of confession from Psalm 51:1–2: 'Have mercy on me, O God, because of your unfailing love. Because of your great compassion, blot out the stain of my sins. Wash me clean from my guilt. Purify me from my sin.' The words from the Lord's Prayer in Matthew 6:12 could also be used: 'Forgive us our sins, as we have forgiven those who sin against us.'

- Sit back, relax and close your eyes. Imagine the scene as someone reads the monologue.

Monologue

I come from a military family, and my grandfather was Ahithophel, one of David's closest advisers. Not surprisingly, the husband chosen for me was from a military background—Uriah the Hittite. My father, Eliam, and my husband were among David's 37 'mighty men', selected from his fighting force for both their military skill and their devotion to David. These men were our heroes, men of outstanding bravery.

David inspired their loyalty and, with him, they were victorious against our enemies, performing great exploits in his name. For many years they had lived as fugitives with David; now that he was king and had a life of plenty, he ensured that his men were rewarded. Uriah, my husband, was given a home next to David's palace in Jerusalem. There I lived as wife of one of the most respected military leaders in Israel. My husband was faithful to his king, his men and all Israel.

Uriah was often fighting away from home. That spring, when our lives were irrevocably changed, he had gone into battle with Joab. They had destroyed the Amorites and were besieging Rabbah. Increasingly, so Uriah told me, Joab was commanding the army on behalf of David, the king preferring to stay in the comfort of Jerusalem.

One evening, as dusk was falling, I took a bath on the roof of the house and then retired inside to rest and sleep. Earlier that day I had made the sacrifices to make me ceremonially clean, exactly one week after the cessation of my period, as was required by the law.

The safety of my husband, father and grandfather were never far from my mind, so when there was a knock on the door and a request for me to come immediately before King David, I presumed that there was news from the campaign—news so significant to me that it could not wait until morning. I trembled with anxiety, my heart pounding and my throat dry.

'Is there information about my relatives?' I asked the messengers as they took me into the palace. Why did they look at me in that way as they told me that there was no news? Then, rather than taking me to an official room, they told me that David wished to see me in his private chamber. My confusion was replaced by absolute clarity the moment the door into David's chamber was opened: the look on David's face, his attire, the dim lighting, the waft of perfume, the prepared bed. There was no shadow of a doubt why I had been called to the king.

'I saw you bathing, Bathsheba. I have never laid eyes on anybody more beautiful.'

I attempted a protest: 'You know who my husband is, and my father and grandfather.'

'I know,' he replied.

In the days ahead, I asked myself whether there had been any choice: could I have run from the room, as Joseph had when Potiphar's wife attempted to seduce him? What would have happened if I had refused? *Could* anyone refuse the king's request? Can I excuse myself by saying I had been overawed? Was the fault with me for not bathing in more private conditions, beneath a canopy? It certainly wasn't rape: I acquiesced and slept with him. There was not a woman in Israel who did not admire our handsome, courageous and talented king—this man of battle who could also make music and write songs that stirred the heart; this gentle man of strength. Perhaps we all loved him at one level or another. But David had a flaw: in his success he had put his comfort and pleasure before his people, before his God. I had been wronged by David, but I had not put up a fight. I was not without blame.

Back home, I heard nothing from the king. I began to hope that I could bury the hurt and shame deep within my heart, that I could keep our guilty secret hidden from everyone, especially from Uriah, and that our life could, at least superficially, carry on much as before. It was not to be. I waited for my next period. One day late... a week late... and still I waited, until I was convinced—I was carrying David's child. The adultery could no longer be hidden, for a baby had been conceived during my husband's absence. Could David somehow offer me some protection?

I sent a message to the king. No reply. For how many weeks could this secret remain my own? Then I heard that my husband was in Jerusalem because he had been summoned by David to update the king on the progress of the battle. I understood David's scheme and started to make my own, arranging for food and drink to be prepared and getting myself ready for Uriah's appearance later that day. How would I look him in the eyes?

I did not have to: he did not come. I waited throughout the second day, waited until late at night, but no Uriah. I knew the heart of my husband. He would put his men before his personal comfort and pleasure. My husband would not eat luxuriously and lie with his wife while his men were living and sleeping out in the open. What a contrast to David! Uriah, it seemed, would not even enter his house in consideration of the deprivations his men were undergoing.

I was never to see my husband again. I heard the next day that he had returned to join the Israelite army; a week later, I received news that he had died in battle. Uriah had been among those in the front line where the fighting was fiercest, when they had come under attack. He was in the wrong place at the wrong time—or was it the right place at the right time? Was it mere chance that Uriah had been in the front line or had he been placed there on somebody's command?

I was inconsolable, for Uriah had been a good man. His death had given me life, saved me from adultery's death sentence; I was not worthy of such a price. I fasted and mourned deeply for seven days. On the eighth day, I was brought to the palace and there I was made David's wife. Of course there were rumours, which only increased when a son was born to us just seven months later.

Adapting to life among the other wives and concubines was not easy; their hostility and their arrogant children troubled me. My husband called for me often and, flawed as I now knew him to be, my heart opened to him and his to me. One evening he told me that he had received a visit from Nathan, the prophet. God had revealed to Nathan the sordid events of the last year;[28] David was broken, humbled, repentant and sad,[29] so very sad that night.

The next day I noticed that our son was unwell. Oh, how quickly he deteriorated! I barely left him, holding him close, doing all I could for him; I scarcely ate or slept. David, in his way, did all he could for our son too: he prayed and fasted, begging the Lord to preserve our baby's life. I heard that he lay before the Lord in utter humility and brokenness, refusing food, refusing comfort.

One week later, I watched my son pass from this life, his pale shrunken form like alabaster as he lay in my arms, growing cold. Still I held him, unable to move, until I felt him being lifted gently from me. I looked up. 'Where is David?' I asked.

'He is worshipping in the Lord's house,' I was told.

David came to me later that day and held me to him; together we wept for the child that we had loved and lost, the child born of our sin.

Reflection and discussion

■ Did any words or phrases in the monologue stand out for you?

■ In the monologue, Bathsheba considers whether she could have resisted David, and concludes, 'I had been wronged by David, but I had not put up a fight. I was not without blame.' It is easy to excuse our behaviour and to justify ourselves, easy not to make a true assessment of what is going on in our heads and hearts. We read in Jeremiah 17:9–10, 'The heart is deceitful above all things and beyond cure. Who can understand it? "I the Lord search the heart and examine the mind, to reward each person according to their conduct, according to what their deeds deserve"' (NIV). What could Bathsheba have done, if anything, that would have honoured God? Because we cannot always gauge what is going on in our own hearts, Christian fellowship, where there is openness and accountability, can be helpful. Share your experiences of this. Would it be beneficial for you to have a prayer partner or mentor?

■ This story is a warning to us, showing how vulnerable we are to temptation. David, the popular, successful and strong leader, decided not to accompany his men into battle (in effect, abandoning his God-given purpose), staying instead in the luxury of his palace. He must have been understandably battle-weary by this stage in his life. However, it was the start of a slippery slope leading to his spiritual and moral defeat. David misused his power to commit adultery, to manipulate events and finally to arrange Uriah's death. 'But the Lord was displeased with what David had done' (2 Samuel 11:27). Perhaps you have experienced or witnessed the fall of godly individuals and the misuse of their position. Do you think that, as in David's case (in not accompanying his men), an initial misjudgement or error led to the downfall?

- Read Jesus' words in Matthew 5:21–22 and 27–30. Jesus uses hyperbole (exaggeration) to make the point that all our outer actions stem from within, and this is the human problem. In Isaiah 64:6 we read, 'We are all infected and impure with sin. When we display our righteous deeds, they are nothing but filthy rags. Like autumn leaves, we wither and fall, and our sins sweep us away like the wind.' Meditate on the following paraphrase of Romans 8:3–4: 'We aren't saved from sin's grasp by knowing the commandments of God, because we can't and don't keep them, but God put into effect a different plan to save us. He sent his own Son in a human body like ours—except that ours are sinful—and destroyed sin's control over us by giving himself as a sacrifice for our sins. So now we can obey God's laws if we are led by the Holy Spirit and no longer obey the old evil nature within us' (LB). Discuss how, in practice, this is different from 'trying' to be inwardly pure. How can we build the strong foundations described by Jesus in the parable of the wise and foolish builders (Matthew 7:24–27)?
- This is also a story about repentance and forgiveness. In your own time, read 2 Samuel 12:1–14, which tells how the Lord sent the prophet Nathan to rebuke David. David confessed, 'I have sinned against the Lord' and Nathan replied, 'The Lord has forgiven you.' We are promised the same response from God, 'If we confess our sins to him, he is faithful and just to forgive us our sins and to cleanse us from all wickedness' (1 John 1:9). David took what rightfully belonged to another. Are there ways in which we do the same, such as taking more than our fair share of the world's resources?

- God called on Nathan to challenge David by means of a parable. We may need to challenge others at times, so how should this be done? Bear in mind Luke 6:41–42 and Galatians 6:1–3.
- Turn to David's words of confession, found in Psalm 51. These are wonderful words for us to use in prayer when we know that we have failed God and others. What did David recognise about himself and about God? 'The sacrifice you desire is a broken spirit. You will not reject a broken and repentant heart, O God' (v. 17). David and Bathsheba found this to be true amid their grief and in their future. How have you found these words to be true? David did not dwell on his wrongdoing; he knew that he was forgiven and that his life could move forward. Sometimes we can find it hard to forgive ourselves, even when we know that God has forgiven us. If you are able, share times when this has been the case for you, and pray for one another.
- In spite of prayer and fasting, the child did not live, and his death was heartbreaking. Have there been times when the answer to your prayers has been 'no'? If you are able, share the experience. Pray for those known to you who have experienced sorrow and grief. Pray that, like David, they will be able to come to terms with what has happened (see 2 Samuel 12:19–24) and continue to worship God. Pray that, like Bathsheba, they will be comforted.
- Refer to the prayer at the start of this study. You may like to finish by saying the Lord's Prayer.

Conclusion

Take time to pray through your findings. What might God be saying to you? Is anything particularly relevant to your life at the moment? Write down what you have learnt and refer back to it regularly in the days ahead so that it becomes part of your thinking, reacting and general outlook.

Bathsheba (Part 2)

Introduction

- Read 2 Samuel 12:24–25; 1 Kings 1:7–31; 2:13–25.
  You may like to read some of the verses before the
  monologue and the rest of the verses after it.

- Ask God to speak to you through this episode. You
  could use the words from Zechariah's prayer in Luke
  1:68–70: 'Praise the Lord, the God of Israel, because
  he has visited and redeemed his people. He has sent
  us a mighty Saviour from the royal line of his servant
  David, just as he promised through the holy prophets
  long ago.'

- Sit back, relax and close your eyes. Imagine the scene as
  someone reads the monologue.

Monologue

David returned to fighting with his men.[30] He also sought to
ease my pain through his love and tenderness. How merciful
and gracious is our God: I became pregnant and we had a
son, Solomon. It was evident from the start that Solomon was
special in the Lord's eyes. Once more, Nathan, our trusted
friend and adviser as well as prophet, came to see us. Once
again the Lord had spoken to Nathan, and this time the
prophecy concerned Solomon, whom Nathan called Jedidiah,

'beloved of the Lord'—a prophetic name signifying our son's special position. Solomon grew in wisdom, finding favour in his father's and in God's eyes. David promised me that one day he would give his throne to Solomon, the son he could trust, the son who followed the Lord's ways.

We were blessed with a further three sons: Shammua, Shobab and Nathan.[31] I aimed to bring them all up to be like their father—men after God's heart. As much as possible, I tried to keep them away from the poisonous jealousies in the royal household. Instead, I taught them wisdom and humility, stressing their responsibilities as well as their rights.

Those were troubled years for David, for, as Nathan had prophesied,[32] the sons of his other wives brought him much grief. They schemed against each other and their father. For a time we had to seek safety away from Jerusalem.[33] In spite of everything, David hoped, trusted, persevered and worshipped: 'The Lord is my rock and my fortress and my deliverer, my God, my rock, in whom I take refuge, my shield, and the horn of my salvation, my stronghold and my refuge, my saviour; you save me from violence. I call upon the Lord, who is worthy to be praised, and I am saved from my enemies.'[34]

My husband was ageing, worn out by strife and unending personal sorrow. However, more trouble was still to come: the son next in line to the throne, Adonijah, conspired against his father, claiming to be king. Adonijah took with him the military support of Joab and the priestly support of Abiathar. Solomon, alone among David's sons, was not invited to Adonijah's coronation; nor were Zadok the priest, Nathan the prophet, Beniah and those other powerful, loyal, mighty men who would only ever follow David's personal commands. Treachery was afoot.

Nathan requested an audience with me in the palace. With urgency he declared that, unless we took immediate action, my life and Solomon's life would be taken. Nathan had a God-inspired plan: I would go to David and inform him that, even though he had always said that Solomon should reign after him, Adonijah had been made king. Nathan, too, would seek an audience with the king and confirm my words.

Although my beauty had faded, David's love for me had remained constant. As I bowed before him, my husband asked me what I wanted, so I recounted the events: Joab had defected to Adonijah and, at that very moment, there was feasting to celebrate the crowning of Adonijah. I spoke to David of his promise that Solomon would be king after him. I gently pointed out that all Israel would be waiting for David's response: did he support Adonijah or not? If he did not speak, his silence would be seen as support for Adonijah. Without a doubt, Solomon and I would be put to death once David had died and could no longer protect us.

Nathan entered the room, as planned, and I left, pacing up and down in great anxiety, knowing that David's response to Nathan's words would seal my beloved Solomon's destiny. When I was called back in, I listened with relief as David spoke words of hope and security, not only for us, but for all of Israel: 'As surely as the Lord lives, who has rescued me from every danger, your son Solomon will be the next king and will sit on my throne this very day, just as I vowed to you before the Lord, the God of Israel.'[35]

I fell down before David in loyalty and gratitude, my face to the ground, reverently acknowledging David as my lord, the king.

How fragile life is; so much can change in one day! David seemed to gain vitality for one last time. From his bed, he quickly gave orders for three men to be brought into his presence: Zadok the priest, Nathan the prophet, and Benaiah, one of the mighty men who had served him with such devotion. They were to gather the men who were loyal to David; Solomon was to ride on the king's mule, as a sign of David's favour, to Gihon, the spring east of Jerusalem. Our son would be anointed there by Zadok and Nathan; trumpets would be blown and Solomon would be proclaimed the king of Israel. After that, Solomon was to be brought to the palace to sit on David's throne.

That day, all this came to pass. The city was filled with such joy that it felt as if the walls themselves were shouting with excitement. Proudly I watched as my son sat on his father's throne. Solomon's responsibilities started immediately: Adonijah, his half-brother, would need to be dealt with decisively. I was pleased to see that Solomon showed himself to be merciful and wise. He decreed that Adonijah would be given one more chance; if he proved loyal to Solomon, he would live.[36] Perhaps Solomon, in offering forgiveness, had brought peace to David's household; how I hoped so.

My husband had little time left on this earth and, knowing the end was near, he called Solomon to him and shared the wisdom he had gained from many experiences, both good and bad. David implored our son to follow the laws of Moses, God's ways, so that he would prosper and all would go well in his kingdom.

Although expected, David's death caused us immense pain. While we grieved, there was much work for Solomon to do, for David had instructed him to deal with his father's enemies and reward his friends.[37] I tried to support Solomon whenever I could, so when Adonijah asked to see me, I saw it as an opportunity to strengthen the peaceful relationship that he had been offered by Solomon. I wanted to trust Adonijah, yearned for there to be harmony, so I listened to his request.

Adonijah wanted to be given Abishag, the Shunammite, as his wife. Abishag was the beautiful young woman who had cared for my husband as his health faded.

There was a long pause as I assessed the situation. Perhaps there was no hidden agenda: I would work for peace and I would go to Solomon. How blessed I was in my son: his affection and respect for me were evident to all. As soon as I said that I had a request, Solomon promised to meet it, such was his trust in me and his desire to give me pleasure. I explained the situation—but what a change then came over Solomon. Enraged, he cried, 'Can you not see what is really going on? Adonijah is David's elder son. Asking for Abishag from the king's harem is symbolic; it is a challenge. You may as well have just asked me to give my kingdom to Adonijah. I have no choice now, for the Lord has established *me* and *my* descendants on David's throne: Adonijah must die.'

How naive I had been! It was a dark day but the actions were necessary for Solomon to establish himself and his kingdom. The loyal Benaiah was sent to kill Adonijah as well as Joab, who had been my husband's great but brutal military leader for so long before he had turned traitor.

My son was now surrounded by trusted men. He loved the Lord, acted wisely and his kingdom flourished.

Reflection and discussion

- Did any words or phrases in the monologue stand out for you?
- We see God's grace and tenderness in this narrative. Bathsheba was blessed with four sons, one of whom, Solomon, was given the additional name Jedidiah, meaning 'beloved of the Lord'. There are several other occasions in the Bible

when babies or children are especially favoured by God with giftedness, a special purpose, strength, wisdom or a deep relationship with God. Who comes to your mind? Observing the favour of God bestowed on others can be difficult. Share any experiences of this. David's family was rife with jealousies. How can we avoid this in our homes and communities? We read in Deuteronomy 10:17, 'For the Lord your God is... the mighty and awesome God, who shows no partiality and cannot be bribed.' How do you reconcile this verse with the description of Solomon as 'beloved of the Lord'?

■ God's love and grace reach out to each one of us; in that sense, we are all 'beloved of the Lord': 'For we know how dearly God loves us, because he has given us the Holy Spirit to fill our hearts with his love' (Romans 5:5). Share times when you have doubted that you are 'beloved of the Lord', perhaps because of difficult circumstances. By contrast, there may have been times when you have been especially aware of God's love, grace, faithfulness and tenderness. Describe these times to each other. Take time during the week to meditate on Romans 8:38–39: 'Nothing can ever separate us from God's love' (v. 38). You may also like to read Isaiah 49:14–16, 'I have written your name on the palms of my hands' (v. 16).

■ Many of David's unruly sons brought him sorrow. Perhaps we know those who have been grieved deeply by their children. Pray that they, like David, will be able to worship God, even in their pain, and that they will find the Lord to be their rock, fortress, deliverer, refuge, shield, salvation, stronghold and saviour (2 Samuel 22:1–4). Which of these descriptions has special significance for you? Encourage one another by explaining why this is so.

- David spoke positive words of faith and trust in God, as we see in 2 Samuel 22 and in many of the Psalms. Our health and well-being are responsive to the words we speak to ourselves (and to others), as well as to our perspective and outlook on life. In Proverbs 15:15 we read, 'For the despondent, every day brings trouble; for the happy heart, life is a continual feast', and in Proverbs 12:18, 'the words of the wise bring healing'. How can we speak words of strength and healing to ourselves and into our lives?
- Bathsheba used her influence with both David and Solomon for good. Where do you have God-given influence? Bathsheba had to tread the difficult line between helpfulness and interference. How can we achieve this balance?
- In the monologue, Bathsheba comments on the fragility of life. Solomon showed that he was only too aware of this when he wrote, 'Remember that nothing is certain in this life' (Ecclesiastes 7:14). Read Jesus' words in Matthew 6:25–34. Life may be uncertain, but Jesus stresses that we have a heavenly Father who knows all our needs. How do we seek the kingdom of God above all else and thus benefit from the promise in verse 33?
- Solomon sought peace with his half-brother, Adonijah, offering him mercy and forgiveness. We read, 'A gentle answer turns away wrath, but a harsh word stirs up anger' (Proverbs 15:1, NIV). Share your experiences of this.
- However, Adonijah found another way to try to claim the throne, attempting to use Bathsheba to manipulate Solomon. Perhaps it was her desire for peace that prevented Bathsheba from seeing the true situation. A longing for peace can result in naivety; some situations cannot be resolved without confrontation. Turning a blind

eye can, in reality, be disastrous (see 1 Kings 1:5–6). Can you give examples of this from history or from your life experiences?

■ Solomon saw through Adonijah's plan and had to take hard but necessary action. Are there times when you have had to act decisively like this, or have seen it done in family, church or community life? If you are able, describe these occasions to one another. Solomon, from his experiences, said that there is 'a time to tear down and a time to build up' (Ecclesiastes 3:3).

Conclusion

Take time to pray through your findings. What might God be saying to you? Is anything particularly relevant to your life at the moment? Write down what you have learnt and refer back to it regularly in the days ahead so that it becomes part of your thinking, reacting and general outlook.

Esther (Part 1)

Introduction

- Read Esther 2:1–18; 4:1–14. You may like to read the verses from Esther 2 before the monologue, and the verses from Esther 4 after the monologue.

- Ask God to speak to you through this episode. You could use the words from Colossians 1:9–10: 'We ask God to give you complete knowledge of his will and to give you spiritual wisdom and understanding. Then... your lives will produce every kind of good fruit. All the while, you will grow as you learn to know God better and better.'

- Sit back, relax and close your eyes. Imagine the scene as someone reads the monologue.

Monologue

My letter is written and, with its seal, the outcome of this chapter in my people's lives is concluded. In this letter I have added my authority as queen to that of my cousin, Mordecai. My people are to establish a further annual festival—the festival of Purim. By now, the epistle will have been copied and sent to 127 provinces stretching from India to Ethiopian, right across the empire of my husband, King Xerxes. We are to celebrate each year with feasts and gifts, supporting the poor among us. We will remember how we were delivered from the evil plans of our enemies that would have led to the annihilation of our people; even as queen, I would not have escaped.[38]

I was not born into a family of nobility; my parents died young and my cousin, Mordecai, raised me. He was a father to me, a source of strength and wisdom. Our family descends from the tribe of Benjamin and had been exiled from Jerusalem to Babylon. Mordecai lived and worked in the fortress of Susa, from where King Xerxes reigned.

I suppose my story starts with the fall of Queen Vashti, who was banished from the king's presence for failing to entertain his guests.[39] As a result, the king's agents travelled to every province on a quest to find the most beautiful virgins and take them into the royal harem. It is true that I had seen men turn their heads to look at me for as long as I could remember, but it still came as a shock when I found that I had been summoned by the royal officials. My cousin's grave face revealed his fears for me and I clung to every word of his advice. We could not stand against the king's plans; the most Mordecai could do was to prepare me mentally and spiritually for the life ahead of me. He counselled me to keep quiet about my nationality and family background.

Once in the harem, I realised I was fortunate compared to many of the girls who had been taken far from their homes and loved ones. I knew that Mordecai walked in front of the court of the harem each day, stopping to find out how I was and what was happening to me.

Hegai, the eunuch in charge of the harem, seemed to show me particular kindness. It appeared that he felt I had great potential and, in addition to the twelve months of beauty treatment that we all received, I was given a special regime, moved into the best part of the harem and assigned seven maids to attend to me.

At the end of the year, each of us would spend a night with the king and then be taken to the second harem, reserved for the concubines. That one night's encounter with the king would determine our future; if a girl pleased him, the king might ask for her again by name. So my preparation continued—with oil, myrrh, perfumes and cosmetics—until the day came when I was told that I would be going to the king that evening. We were permitted to take whatever we wanted with us. Nervously, I asked Hegai for his advice and followed his recommendations. I was aware of everyone's admiration, but would I win the king's favour?

No doubt my cousin held me in his prayers that night while King Xerxes held me in his arms. It was not long before I was asked to attend the king again, and then again and again. The rumour spread throughout the palace that the king had fallen in love with me. Had his feelings for me really moved beyond those of physical attraction and passion? Then came the day when the king decreed that I was to be made queen in place of Vashti. A celebratory banquet was prepared in my name and the king ensured that his empire celebrated with him. While all this attention was being lavished upon me, my cousin advised me, just as he always had done, keeping me grounded and enabling me to fulfil my role with wisdom, humility, integrity and a quiet confidence. How I was to need those qualities in the days ahead!

It was not long before I had my first opportunity to use my position for the benefit of others. Mordecai, who had now become a palace official, was sitting at the king's gates, waiting for his services to be called upon. He heard of a plot concocted by two of the king's eunuchs, who were guards at the gates—a plan to assassinate King Xerxes. My cousin immediately told me and I was able to report it to the king and save his life. Mordecai's act of service was written down in the king's records.[40]

However, Mordecai's loyalty to the king went unrewarded and my cousin soon found himself in a difficult situation. Haman, of Amalekite descent and hence an enemy of my people, became the king's right-hand man. My husband could see no faults in this arrogant man and fed his ego by commanding that all should bow down to Haman. I was not surprised that my cousin refused; true to his faith, he believed that people should bow down only before God. Mordecai was not a man to compromise and, in spite of the servants' warnings, he continued to hold his ground. Eventually, Haman was told of this defiance and went to the palace gates himself, and sure enough, Mordecai did not bow down to him. Haman's fury at my cousin's attitude was great. I feared for Mordecai's life.[41]

Little did I realise what scheming was going on behind the scenes as Haman manipulated the king, turning him against my people. The first I knew of it was when my maids and the eunuchs told me that Mordecai was at the entrance to the king's gate, clothed in sackcloth, weeping bitterly. Desperate to speak to Mordecai, I ordered clothes to be sent to him so that he could enter the gate. He refused, so I sent my trustworthy eunuch, Hathach, to find out from him exactly what was happening.

Hathach returned with Mordecai's report of Haman's terrible plan of revenge on our people. Haman had persuaded the king that we were a danger to him and the empire because we refused to give up our customs and disobeyed the king's laws. Therefore, we must be destroyed. What terrifyingly clever logic! Hathach handed me a copy of the edict ordering the elimination of all my people throughout the empire, a pronouncement sealed with the king's ring. The ruling was binding. Haman had offered to pay the king handsomely to eradicate us and had chosen by lot the day for our destruction. The king, blinded to Haman's evil intention, had agreed; decrees had been sent through the empire, ordering massacre and plunder.

Mordecai, Hathach informed me, believed that I should go to the king and plead for my people; it was our only hope. I instructed Hathach to tell Mordecai that this was impossible. Surely he knew that to approach the king without being summoned would result in death, unless the king chose to hold out his golden sceptre. Besides, I was beginning to think that the king was losing interest in me; a month had passed since he had last asked for me.

But my cousin, who saw situations in black-and-white, perceived a spiritual battle beneath all this human pride and cunning. His reply was forthright: surely I realised that my identity could not remain hidden, that I too would be killed. My position in the royal household would offer no protection. Mordecai saw providence at work, believing that I had been made queen for such a time as this, in order to save my people. If I refused to play my part, I would perish; but even if that should be, he believed that somehow our people would be delivered from our enemies, as in bygone days.

Reflection and discussion

■ Did any words or phrases in the monologue stand out for you?

■ God is not mentioned by name in the book of Esther. However, in every section of the narrative his presence, guiding hand and sovereignty are clearly seen, as is the outworking of the faith of his chosen ones. Also very much in evidence is the spiritual battle between good and evil. Recall other times in history when the battle between good and evil has come to the forefront in world events. Are we aware of the underlying conflict and tension within our own spiritual lives? Read Ephesians 6:10–17 and Romans 7:21–25.

- The celebrations at Purim involved not only feasting and exchanging gifts, but also supporting the poor. Suggest ideas for how we can do something similar during our key celebrations (such as Christmas), as individuals, churches and communities.

- Do you know people who, like Mordecai, have taken on the responsibility of looking after and bringing up other people's children? Take time to pray for them and for organisations known to you that support children orphaned by disease and war.

- Mordecai was a source of strength and wisdom to Esther, both when she was growing up and in her role as queen; he had instilled in her the values that she would need in her adult life. Are you in a position to support any young adults with advice and prayer? If you are a young adult yourself, are there areas where you need wisdom and advice? Who could support you?

- Esther had no choice but to enter the harem; acceptance of the situation was the only way forward for both her and Mordecai. Share times in your life when you have been given grace to accept difficult circumstances. Perhaps you currently find yourself in a situation that is hard to accept; you may wish to benefit from the prayers and support of others.

- We sense that, even in the difficult atmosphere of the harem, God was with Esther, as she soon found favour in the eyes of Hegai, the eunuch in charge. Share times when you have experienced God's care during circumstances not of your own choosing.
- Esther had both an outer beauty and an inner beauty. What qualities do you see in others that give them an inner beauty? Compare your response to Galatians 5:22–23.
- Another of Esther's qualities was her humility: she was ready to ask for and take Hegai's advice. Why can it be so hard for us to seek and take advice? Jesus talks a lot about pride and humility—for example, in the parable of the Pharisee and the tax collector in Luke 18:9–14. In Matthew 11:29, Jesus describes himself as 'humble and gentle'; in him we find 'rest for our souls'. How have you experienced this rest? Being in humble and gentle company is indeed restful, whereas being in abrasive and arrogant company is quite the opposite. Share incidents in which you have found this to be true.
- Mordecai was a man who refused to compromise his faith; he would bow down to the Lord and no other (see Exodus 20:5). As a result, Haman was enraged and planned a terrible revenge on all the people of God. Are there times when we have needed to stand our ground without compromise? What were the consequences?
- Mordecai challenges Esther quite strongly at the end of this monologue. Do we ever feel able to challenge those to whom we are close? In what circumstances? Have we ever been challenged by others? How did we respond? Proverbs 15:31 reads, 'If you listen to constructive criticism, you will be at home among the wise.'

■ Refer back to the prayer at the start of this study. Consider how you are producing fruit and getting to know God better.

Conclusion

Take time to pray through your findings. What might God be saying to you? Is anything particularly relevant to your life at the moment? Write down what you have learnt and refer back to it regularly in the days ahead so that it becomes part of your thinking, reacting and general outlook.

Esther (Part 2)

Introduction

- Read Esther 4:14—5:7; 7:1—8:8. You may like to read the verses from Esther 4 and 5 before the monologue, and the verses from Esther 7 and 8 after the monologue.

- Ask God to speak to you through this episode. You could use the words of Romans 15:13: 'I pray that God, the source of hope, will fill you completely with joy and peace because you trust in him. Then you will overflow with confident hope through the power of the Holy Spirit.'

- Sit back, relax and close your eyes. Imagine the scene as someone reads the monologue.

Monologue

'Perhaps you were made queen for such a time as this.'

I could not get Mordecai's words out of my mind. It was clear what I had to do: I must go to the king, although to do so was against the law. Whatever the outcome, whether I lived or died, I would do all that was in my power to save my people—but I would need to know not only that I and my maids had fasted, but also that my cousin and the people of Susa had joined us in three days of intercession. Hathach took my message to Mordecai and returned with his answer: my cousin was satisfied with my response and had left immediately to call our people to prayer and fasting.

I knew that I needed to act cautiously, carefully and shrewdly, for my enemy, Haman, was powerful. I had three days in which to plan my move. On the third day I rose early, asking my maids to take the utmost care in preparing me to approach the king. Adorned in royal robes, I waited in the inner palace court, where I could be seen from the king's throne. My heart thumped wildly, although outwardly I endeavoured to look calm. I looked up and caught his eye. Surely I was not mistaken: there was a look of pleasure on his face when he saw me. I waited, my eyes fixed on the sceptre. Slowly he lifted his hand and pointed the golden sceptre towards me. My life was temporarily spared. I walked forward and touched the very end of the sceptre.

The king's words to me were undoubtedly words of love; my fear of having lost favour subsided as he asked me what I wanted, promising me even half of his kingdom. I made my request: would he and Haman join me at a banquet that I had arranged especially for them?

It was not an easy dinner for me, watching the egotistical Haman and listening to his smooth words, but I had to play my part and keep to my plan. So I plied them with food and wine and waited for the king to address me. After what seemed an age, he asked me what it was that I wanted; I could request anything, absolutely anything. Yet the time was not right; I needed the king to be even more anxious to hear what I had to say, even more desirous to please me. So I merely invited them to return for another banquet the next day, promising to give him an answer then.

The following day, I made arrangements for a second sumptuous feast to be prepared. The most extraordinary message came to me, one that was to lift my spirits and give me confidence for the task ahead. Haman was leading Mordecai, dressed in the king's robes, around the city on the king's horse, which was adorned with the royal headdress. Apparently the king, sleeping badly, had asked for his diary of days to be read to him and had been reminded of the great service done to him by my cousin. On discovering that Mordecai had gone unrewarded, the king had sought Haman's advice, as was his custom. How should a man be honoured by the king? Haman, expecting that the king wished to reward him, had then planned the tribute. What a humiliation for Haman to find himself required to lead his enemy around the city! His downfall had commenced.[42]

I knew that tonight was the moment to tell the king of my identity and to fight for my people's cause. Once again, I waited for the king to take the lead. This time, I was less fearful, for I carried in my head the picture of my cousin receiving honour from the king. So when my husband asked me what I would like, I was able to pour out my story: *my* life was to be taken and *my* people destroyed. The king was outraged: who would dare to plot against his queen? He had still not connected my words with Haman's proposal, sealed with his own signet ring. In fury, he asked me who was responsible for such an outrageous scheme. I turned to Haman, pointed at him, and said in a low voice, 'This vile enemy, Haman.'

The king stormed out of the room into the palace garden and I remained reclining silently on the couch while Haman begged for his life. In desperation, he fell across me, the merciless one pleading for mercy. At that moment, my husband returned and, seeing Haman touching me, his anger knew no bounds. Accusing Haman of assault, he ordered his immediate death. One of the eunuchs told the king of the gallows that Haman had had constructed, where he had planned to have Mordecai hung.[43] The king ordered that Haman be hung on these very gallows.

The king channelled his cooling fury into action: he instructed that Haman's estate should be given to me. When I explained my relationship to Mordecai, the king ordered that my cousin should replace Haman as his foremost adviser, giving him his signet ring. I entrusted Mordecai with the management of Haman's estate.

Our safety was secured, but not that of our people. Once again, I dared approach the king, but gone was my reserve; in truth I fell at his feet, weeping and pleading with him to stop the evil plot hatched by Haman. Once again, I saw the golden sceptre stretched towards me and, collecting myself, I rose. Carefully, I made my request: 'If I have found favour with you, and if you believe it is right and are in agreement, may Haman's order be withdrawn; for how could I bear to see my people massacred?'

There was a silence—a silence in which a plan to save our people was being conceived. Finally, my husband said that, although he could not revoke an edict that he had sealed, he could give permission for a further decree to be sent out to the 127 provinces, with words of our choosing and signed with his seal.

Straight away, Mordecai prepared a *diktat* in which our people were given permission to do all that they could to defend themselves, their families and properties. What rejoicing and celebration filled Susa and the provinces as the news spread! All of a sudden we were a feared and honoured people.[44]

So it came to pass that our enemies throughout the empire and in Susa itself were destroyed, including Haman's sons.

Mordecai's position was powerful; he was held in such awe and respect by all the governors of the provinces that they assisted our people in defending themselves.

We are now safe. My people will remember this deliverance by holding an annual celebration in which we feast, giving gifts to each other and to the poor. Our despair and mourning have been replaced by light, gladness, honour and joy.[45]

Reflection and discussion

- Did any words or phrases in the monologue stand out for you?
- Mordecai sent the message to Esther, 'Perhaps you were made queen for such a time as this.' Although Mordecai made no specific reference to God, his comment suggests his belief that Esther had been made queen for a purpose. This belief must have sustained him whenever he thought of Esther living in a harem. Share experiences when you have been in a certain position at a certain time, which has served an unforeseen purpose.
- Esther was placed in a position of influence. She might have been expected to stay on the fringes of political and religious life, yet she broke with the norm and, finding her voice and purpose, used her position for the benefit of others. Pray for those in positions of influence, both locally and nationally, that they will have integrity, that they will hold back from the temptation to be self-seeking and self-protective, and that they will do all in their power to help the vulnerable. Have there been times in your life when you have found that you had a voice worthy of being heard, and have discovered a new purpose? God may place us in situations where we can be his voice. Can

you relate any examples? We read in Ecclesiastes 3:7 that there is a time to be quiet and a time to speak: we need the leading of the Holy Spirit to prompt the appropriate response.

■ Esther means 'star', and her qualities shine through in this story—her beauty, wisdom, humility, sensitivity, careful planning, concern for others and courage in taking action. There may well be times in our lives when we are called to 'shine', not for our own glory but so that God will be praised. Read and meditate on Jesus' words in Matthew 5:14–16. Share your experiences of being a 'light'.

■ In this story we see the interplay between God's sovereignty and human choice, which we may never fully grasp. God set the scene and was working behind the scenes, but Mordecai and Esther chose to act. They did not become inactive or passive in a situation that could have seemed hopeless to them. How, in your life experiences, have you seen the interplay between God's overruling sovereignty and your choices and actions?

■ Esther found a purpose for which she was willing to live or die. In Hebrews 11:32–38 we read that some of the faithful were miraculously delivered when they stood up for God's ways and people (as in the narrative of Esther), yet others suffered dreadfully and were martyred. Pray for those who take huge risks for Christ and the gospel message, and for those who risk their personal well-being because they have found their purpose in fighting for the causes of others. Pray for the motivation and courage to speak out against injustices that concern you.

■ We see the role that fasting and intercession played in preparing Esther to act, and in softening the king's heart. Esther understood that she needed the spiritual support of others. One of the functions of groups of believers is to give mutual support. Are you part of a network like this, and, if so, how has it helped you? Jesus assumed that his followers would fast (Matthew 6:16–18). Share any experiences you have of the value of this spiritual discipline. In your own time you may like to consider Isaiah 58:5–14, in which the Lord describes the kind of 'fasting' that he desires.

- Esther was prompted to hold back from presenting her case to the king during the first feast. Are there times when you have had a prompting from the Holy Spirit that has stopped you from taking action? Share these experiences. At the time, we may not know why we have held back, but it may become clearer at a later point, as it did for Esther when she heard the next day that the tables were turning and that Haman had been ordered by the king to honour Mordecai for saving the king's life.

- The king could not sleep and asked for his diary to be brought to him, leading to his discovery that Mordecai had not been rewarded for saving his life. This resulted in his decision to honour Mordecai, which must have been such an encouragement to Esther. Behind the scenes God was at work, creating exactly the right moment for her to speak. Recall times when you have been encouraged by unexpected changes that God has brought into your life.

- This narrative shows us how much can be achieved through the faithfulness of individuals. Can you suggest Christians you may have read about who changed the lives of many people through their actions? Reading such accounts can be a great encouragement on our faith journey. Read Jesus' words in Matthew 18:19–20.

- God's people knew 'light and gladness and honour and joy' on their deliverance (Esther 8:16, ESV); our deliverer still brings these gifts into our lives. Can we, like David, say, 'The Lord is my light and my salvation—so why should I be afraid?' (Psalm 27:1). Share your experiences of God bringing you light, gladness, joy and honour. Read Isaiah 61:1–3, a prophecy describing the comfort, joy and freedom that the Lord will bring. Jesus refers to himself as the fulfilment of this prophecy, in Luke 4:16–21. How have you experienced Jesus as your comfort, joy and freedom?

Conclusion

Take time to pray through your findings. What might God be saying to you? Is anything particularly relevant to your life at the moment? Write down what you have learnt and refer back to it regularly in the days ahead so that it becomes part of your thinking, reacting and general outlook.

Notes

1   Genesis 12:1–3
2   Genesis 12:7
3   Genesis 13:15
4   Genesis 17:13, 23–27
5   Genesis 17:15–22. This is the first time God explicitly states that the covenant will be fulfilled through Sarah's son.
6   Hebrews 11:11–12
7   Genesis 27:28–29
8   Jacob means both 'heel' and 'deceiver'.
9   Genesis 26:34–35
10 Genesis 47:29–31
11 Genesis 49:8, 10
12 Genesis 42:3–5
13 Genesis 42:35–38
14 Genesis 43:1–14
15 Genesis 44
16 Genesis 45:28
17 Genesis 46:3–4
18 Genesis 46:31–34
19 Numbers 12:15
20 Exodus 4:27–31
21 Exodus 13:21–22
22 Exodus 14:14
23 Exodus 15:1–3, 13
24 Exodus 15:17–18
25 Joshua 3:14–17
26 Joshua 5:1
27 1 Samuel 2:1–2
28 2 Samuel 12:1–14
29 Psalm 51
30 2 Samuel 12:26–31
31 1 Chronicles 3:5
32 2 Samuel 12:10
33 2 Samuel 15:13–16
34 2 Samuel 22:1–4 (ESV)
35 1 Kings 1:29–30
36 1 Kings 1:32–53
37 1 Kings 2:1–12
38 Esther 9:29–32
39 Esther 1:10–22
40 Esther 2:19–23
41 Esther 3
42 Esther 6
43 Esther 5:9–14
44 Esther 8:9–17
45 Esther 8:16

Also by Fiona Stratta

Walking with Gospel Women

Interactive Bible meditations

Imaginative meditation can be a powerful way of attuning ourselves to God's presence, involving as it does the emotions as well as the mind. This book offers a refreshing and inspiring way into Bible study, using meditative monologues based around many of the women of the Gospels. Through a time of guided reflection, we identify with the woman concerned and see what lessons emerge for today as we ponder her story.

Each chapter consists of a monologue, linked Bible passage and discussion material designed to draw out deep communication and group fellowship, as well as transformational learning. While designed primarily for small groups meeting to grow their relationships with God and with each other, the monologues can also be used as a way into silent reflection either for individuals or with larger groups.

ISBN 978 0 85746 010 3   £7.99
Available from your local Christian bookshop or direct from BRF: please visit www.brfonline.org.uk.

Mary

A gospel witness to transfiguration and liberation

Andrew Jones

Mary is arguably the first disciple, and this book explores the different ways she is presented in the Gospels and also in Christian spirituality through history, showing how her significance extends far beyond the Christmas story. As more than just a mother at the manger, Mary can be a pattern for our own discipleship. She is an enduring witness to the central importance of transfiguration and liberation as characteristics of the kingdom of God, which should also be visible in our lives as followers of Jesus today.

Includes group discussion material.

ISBN 978 1 84101 651 1   £8.99
Available from your local Christian bookshop or direct from BRF: please visit www.brfonline.org.uk.

Also from BRF

Hilda of Whitby

A spirituality for now

Ray Simpson

In the dark and turbulent centuries after the Roman occupation of Britain and during the Anglo-Saxon colonisation, the light of heaven still shone through the work and witness of the monastic communities, 'villages of God', which dotted the land. One of the most remarkable figures of those times was Hilda of Whitby. Born and reared among warring pagan tribes, through the influence of Celtic saints and scholars she became a dominant figure in the development of the British Church, above all at the famous Synod where Celtic and Roman Churches came together. Until recently, though, the story of this extraordinary woman has not received much attention.

Published to coincide with the 1400th anniversary of her birth, this book not only explores the drama of Hilda's life and ministry but shows what spiritual lessons we can draw for Christian life and leadership today

ISBN 978 1 84101 728 0   £7.99
Available from your local Christian bookshop or direct from BRF: please visit www.brfonline.org.uk.

Living Liturgies

Transition time resources for services, prayer and conversation with older people

Caroline George

This book offers a creative worship resource for pastoral ministry with those at an often overlooked time of life—the move from independent living to dependency, or from the 'third age' to the 'fourth age' of life. The twelve liturgies—and accompanying reflections for those leading the worship—were developed by Caroline George after many years of working in church and community settings with older people and provide valuable help for those embarking on this ministry, as well as inspiration for those already involved.

Each specially written liturgy uses a simple structure based around a theme to weave together experience, scripture and the assurance of God's love and grace. Conversation is used to connect the theme with past, present and future, leading into prayer and silent reflection with the help of a visual aid.

ISBN 978 0 85746 323 4   £7.99
Available from your local Christian bookshop or direct from BRF: please visit www.brfonline.org.uk.

Also from BRF

Journalling the Bible

40 writing exercises

Corin Child

The spiritual discipline of journalling has become increasingly popular in recent years and this book shows how it can fruitfully overlap with creative writing to provide an original way of engaging with the Bible.

'Bible study' is usually taken to mean 'reading and discussing'—but writing offers a different way of interacting with the text, generating new insights and application even from the most familiar of passages. Journalling the Bible offers 40 writing/journalling exercises that have been tested in workshops around the country, providing an imaginative resource for individual and group work and a refreshingly different way to become better acquainted with scripture.

ISBN 978 1 84101 736 5   £7.99
Available from your local Christian bookshop or direct from BRF: please visit www.brfonline.org.uk.

80 Creative Prayer Ideas

A resource for church and group use

Claire Daniel

Prayer is a vital part of the Christian life but people often struggle with actually getting on and doing it. This book offers 80 imaginative and creative ideas for setting up 'prayer stations', practical ways of praying that involve the senses—touching, tasting, smelling, seeing and hearing, rather than simply reflecting—as we bring our hopes, fears, dreams and doubts to God.

Developed from material tried and tested with small groups, the ideas provide activities ranging from bubble prayers to clay pot prayers (via just about everything else in between), and have been designed to be used with grown-ups of all ages.

ISBN 978 1 84101 688 7   £8.99
Available from your local Christian bookshop or direct from BRF: please visit www.brfonline.org.uk.

Enjoyed

this book?

Write a review—we'd love to hear what you think.
Email: reviews@brf.org.uk

Keep up to date—receive details of our new books as they happen.
Sign up for email news and select your interest groups at:
www.brfonline.org.uk/findoutmore/

Follow us on Twitter @brfonline

By post—to receive new title information by post (UK only), complete the form below and post to: BRF Mailing Lists, 15 The Chambers, Vineyard, Abingdon, Oxfordshire, OX14 3FE

Your Details
Name _____
Address_____
_____
Town/City _____ Post Code _____
Email_____

Your Interest Groups (*Please tick as appropriate)	
☐ Advent/Lent	☐ Messy Church
☐ Bible Reading & Study	☐ Pastoral
☐ Children's Books	☐ Prayer & Spirituality
☐ Discipleship	☐ Resources for Children's Church
☐ Leadership	☐ Resources for Schools

Support your local bookshop
Ask about their new title information schemes.